The Long Voyage Home

R. Lancy Burn

Copyright © 2004 by R. Lancy Burn

All rights reserved.

No part of this publication may be reproduced, stored in a retrieval system or transmtited, in any form or by any means, electronic, mechanical, photocopying, recording or otherwise, without the prior permission of the publishers.

Cover and text designed by Dreux Sawyer

ISBN 0-9745185-2-2

Published by Arseya, LLC
New Vernon, NJ

www.arseya.com

Printed in the United States by The Wall Street Group, Inc.

Contents

Prologue 1

ONE
The Dream Begins 3

TWO
The Big Decisions 19

THREE
Blue Gipsy Readies for Sea 28

FOUR
The End of the Beginning 43

FIVE
How Do You Salvage a Dream? Very Carefully... 65

SIX
Return to Kastrup 89

SEVEN
If at First You Don't Succeed 95

EIGHT
Passage of the Kiel Canal 102

NINE
Trials of the North Sea 121

TEN
Dover Straits and England 128

ELEVEN
The First Leg:
Falmouth to the Canaries 140

TWELVE
Las Palmas, Grand Canary 159

THIRTEEN
Las Palmas to Turn-the-chart-over 164

FOURTEEN
The Cradle of the Deep 178

FIFTEEN
Bahamas Landfall 198

SIXTEEN
Turn Right to Home 208

Epilogue 217

Acknowledgments

It's only fair to thank my Scottish forebears who brought our family to this new and wonderful land called America. They deserve to be recognized and thanked. Salute! and thank you all. I am because of you.

But then, there are others along the paths, rivers and roads of our lives; movers and shakers who actually change the outcome of plans, schemes and dreams.

First and foremost of these would be my loving and patient wife Emily, who is the bravest person I have ever met. She will stay by my side and face anything. She does not waver. She has encouraged me to live a sane life and write since the beginning of our wonderful relationship, and has typed this book a dozen times at least. A loving thank you my dearest Emily.

My grandfather, Arthur Ashley "Pappy" Burn, whose stories of sea and sail inspired me to actually go to sea. I only wish that he could have lived to sail aboard *Blue Gipsy*. Thank you Pappy Burn.

My father who was tough as hell and a little mean but he was proud that one of us finally sailed a boat across that bloody ocean—thanks for the prod Pop.

My mother Billie Burn, to whom, along with Emily, this book is dedicated. Thanks Mom.

Colonel Casey Cason (US Army, deceased), whom I wished could have lived long enough to see this book come into being. A belated thanks to you Casey.

Mr. Porter Thompson along with Col. Cason worked together to draw the plans and lay the keel for this book, and other kindnesses too, that helped me along. Thank you Porter.

Patricia Beichler who snatched this book out of the

fire so to speak. Using her computer and typing skills she managed to salvage mildewed disks, obsolete word processor programs, and lost text—she saved it all and inspired me to get this book into publication. Thank you Pat.

Thanks to all those others, who inadvertently helped this story to be told.

R. Lancy Burn

Prologue

I stood in the cold drizzling rain with a camera clenched between gloved hands, trying my best to get some pictures of the sloop *Blue Gipsy* being launched without ruining everything. I clicked away as the blue-clad workmen moved her into position over the rusty steel rails of the ways, using a farm tractor to tug her this way and that. Finally the tow bar was unhitched and several of the men brought heavy jacks and after placing them around the cradle which supported the boat, proceeded to jack it up high enough to place a small, sturdy, metal trolley under the boat's keel. Next they lowered her onto the trolley and took the jacks away. Finally, with very little to-do, a cable was attached to both ends of the trolley. From a small building came the clash of gears. There were some hand signals and the cable snapped taut, the trolley gave a jerk, and the boat rocked a bit. I held my breath and clicked away. The cable jerked again and *Blue Gipsy* moved steadily down the ways, her keel bit into the icy blue-green water of the Baltic Sea sending little waves rippling away. She slowed and seemed to settle down, rocked gently, then floated free of the cradle. She was born!

I quickly put my camera back into its case. The rain came down heavier as the workmen tied the boat alongside the quay and I heard the little Volvo diesel take its first few breaths before settling into a steady thump like a heartbeat. Suddenly I felt jubilant and a wave of relief flowed through me. A milestone had been passed. The launching was the end of ten years of working, planning and scheming for this very moment; it was the beginning of a voyage. The voyage my grandfather and my father had dreamed of. It was happening and at the moment I couldn't even guess at how soon we would be tried and tested. I couldn't conceive how close we would come to death by freezing or drowning and even nearly loosing my beautiful *Blue Gipsy*. Nor could I guess the breath-taking beauty of sailing through some of the finest sailing winds in the world, the Atlantic tradewinds. This voyage would strengthen us and yet humble us. It would set the elements against us like a pack of wolves, snapping and biting and giving no quarter, no time to think or rest. We had to do our utmost not to lose. Through all this we learned much about ourselves, the wind and sea, and about the sheer joy of sailing. But let's go back to the beginning…of The Long Voyage Home.

CHAPTER ONE
The Dream Begins...

I was born in Charleston, South Carolina on April 4, 1939, the second child of my parents. A sister, born three years before me was the first. When I was nine years old my parents were blessed with another son, the last of the family. My early years were spent in various cities of the Southeast United States, and it was not until I was seven years old did we move to the city of Savannah, Georgia. This is important because it was close to the home of my grandfather. He was living on the sea island of Daufuskie in South Carolina, which was but ten miles up the Intracoastal Waterway from Savannah. My fondest memories are about the island and it was here that I learned to fish, hunt and mess about in boats. It was here that "the dream" was passed on to me.

My grandfather and my father wanted to make a long voyage across the broad Atlantic in a small sailboat. They both had harboured that dream during younger years but because of family pressures or other responsibilities neither of them ever made their dreams come true.

Going further back, I can't help but wonder if the same dream had not been passed on from generation to generation, down through the years before it came into my possession. John Paul Burn, a Scottish cabin boy aboard a German ship probably started it all when he jumped ship in Charleston and hid in a chimney until the ship was safely out of sight. He was from Germany, and it was in the latter half of the 1700's that he made Charleston his new home. I like to think that at times he longed for home and wished to sail back to Germany in his own small boat. It's an interesting thought anyway.

My grandfather was a tall, white haired man close to seventy years old the first time I remember seeing him. He had a thin face with sharp features and laughing blue eyes that matched his bottomless sense of humor. He was the only bonified character that I have ever personally known. In his younger years he had served in the US Army and was stationed on Hilton Head Island, SC during the Spanish American War. The boats to Savannah passed Daufuskie and he became enthralled with the island. After the war he went back to his home in Charleston and in 1913 landed a job with the Lighthouse Service as "Assistant Lighthouse Keeper, Bloody Point Lighthouse, Daufuskie Island. There were two range lights on the island that steered ships up the twisting and tricky Savannah River channel. Later when the channel changed its course and the light discontinued, he purchased the lighthouse and stayed on at Daufuskie taking up fishing and later becoming Magistrate of the Island, a post he held for many years.

He fished with my father in a large ketch-rigged sailing bateau named "Missy." They sailed *Missy* off shore to the shoals out in front of the islands of Hilton Head, Daufuskie and Tybee Island, Georgia. They used handlines to take Spot-tailed Bass, Whiting, Black Fish, Croakers and Flounders, which they would sell to the people on Tybee Island and to the soldiers stationed at Ft. Screven there.

This was during and just after the big depression. Times were hard and cash money scarce, they would trade the fish to the soldiers for items almost impossible to obtain elsewhere such as .22 cartridges and shoes. They both had thrilling stories to tell of the big fish they didn't always land, and of having to sail the old bateau back to the island through storm and squall. I often regret that I never got to sail with my grandfather for he was a real sailor from the days of sail. He did teach me many other things, though.

We could not live on Daufuskie because there was no way for my father to make a decent living with the meager economy of Daufuskie. But life in Savannah wasn't too bad since Daufuskie was close by and became a weekend summer place. I loved to go to my grandfather's house because we would go fishing every day. He was fun to be with and I learned not only how to fish and row a boat but how to splice a line, whistle up the wind and throw the cast net for bait and shrimp. He also gave me my first lesson in moving heavy objects with rollers and pry poles. More often than not we would have to roll the old bateau "off the hill" where the tide had left her before we could go fishing. I learned many lessons and never forgot them.

While waiting for the fish to bite, my grandfather would tell me stories about his younger days. The stories about sailing were my favorites. He would tell me also how he wanted to buy himself a nice little thirty or thirty-two foot sloop and, "sail across that ocean," nodding his head at the horizon to the East…and maybe around the world.

Father was the same height as my grandfather but heavier and stocky built. When he's the age my grandfather was he'll have the same white hair and sharp features and will pass as a twin to him. The blue eyes are there too, along with a quick grin and keen sense of humor. In younger days after the depression he skippered tugs at different times for both the U.S. Corps of Engineers and the tobacco tycoon, R.J. Reynolds. Later he turned to plastering as a trade, which gave him more time at home with his growing family.

    He operated a little tug called the "Flapper" for Mr. Reynolds, hauling building materials to Sapelo Island, Georgia, a retreat he owned, and cattle on and off the Island. He also got in some off shore sailing experience on the large yawl that Reynolds owned going along as deckhand. Once during a voyage from Sapelo to New York, they were caught in a fierce Gulf Stream squall with all sail up and had pulled some rigging loose and broken the mizzen boom. I never tired of hearing how it all happened and how, after repairs at sea, they had carried on to New York. One of my greatest treasures as a boy was a dried flying fish wing that my father had given to me, a momento he'd kept of the trip. He also harboured the dream of some day owning his own small sailboat and making a long voyage as well. This was how the dream was passed on to me.

    Although my father was a plastering contractor in Savannah, he still liked to fish and for several years he owned a 50-foot shrimp boat named *Miss Terry*. In the winter he liked very much to gill net fish and would take me along on these weekend trips to row the boat. One of our nets was six hundred feet long and we would set it out along the marsh and then go back and forth, running it, taking the fish out as they were caught and this meant a lot of hard rowing for me in a heavy ba-dough with a pair of nine-foot oars cut down to 8 feet so the big blades could get a good bite. No easy job for a lad of twelve. We would fish the tide or about six hours before taking up and heading for home. I can remember rowing when the wind was up until I thought my arms were going to break off. They didn't of course and I got strong and could make a boat do anything but stand on its ear with a pair of oars. When winter was over so was the gill net fishing. Too many crabs, sharks and skates to foul the net, but then shrimp season opened and school was out and summer vacation started. I would be on the shrimp boat hauling lines and heading shrimp from sunup 'til sundown and if the catch had been good on into the night. On her I learned how to splice wire and work a windlass and how to keep my feet under me on a heaving deck. I learned a thousand ways to become a seaman. The hours were long and the work was hard, but I thrived on it and I really enjoyed being at sea.

I learned to watch the weather too and to be alert for what was going on around and about the boat. I also learned to recognize and name most of the creatures we hauled up from the sea and the names of all the different kinds of seabirds that followed in our wake. It was a well-rounded education that I received during those summers, but ironically, I had yet to sail my first boat.

I was about fourteen when I went sailing for the first time. I had rowed our old ba-dough up the river one afternoon to do a little marsh combing. The tide was springing, and I would row along and search for what I could find in the way of useful flotsam and jetsam. Usually it was lumber or the like. That day it was a twelve-foot ladder and a stout 12-foot boathook with a bronze fitting on it. I took them aboard and headed for home against a strong ebb tide. I had a good following breeze but it was going to be a long, hard up-hill pull. Suddenly I had an idea. There was a ten-foot square tarp in the boat that we had used to cover the groceries with on the trip from Savannah that very morning, and it would make a perfect downwind sail. Hurriedly I tied the ladder upright in the boat, securing it with bow and stern lines. Then I used fishing line to lash the boathook across the top of the tarp, and after passing a line through the top rung of the ladder, I hoisted the sail up. I had some sheeting problems until I lashed an oar across the bottom of the tarp as well and using the other oar to steer with I sailed home. My father saw me coming and had quite a laugh over my rig. But I was really proud of it. I had managed to launch myself into the fascinating realm of sailing.

My father sold our house out near Hunter Air Field and we moved into a mobile home and parked it out on Whitmarsh Island, East of Savannah. I loved it out there. Plenty of friends and we were in the creeks and rivers constantly, water skiing, fishing and swimming. My cousin had a sailboard that he'd built from plans he found in a Mechanics Illustrated magazine. My Aunt Shorty had sewed up sails from an old orange and white parachute. It was hardly bigger than a surfboard but we had a lot of fun with it. Somehow he became tired of it and passed it on to me. I learned to sail it in every kind of weather. The rougher it was the better I liked it. I suddenly became very aware that the dream of that long voyage had been passed on to me and I was going to do it... I was going to sail across that ocean.

In 1955 we moved our house trailer down to Ft. Lauderdale, Florida. I liked the change and really began to enjoy school. The other kids were from out of town like me, and were much friendlier than the clannish crackers. I liked the fishing and diving in crystal clear water too, it was a great change for me and life was better.

In high school my dream became almost an obsession and was with me constantly. My father took me into his business on weekends and summer vacation and taught me the plastering trade. I didn't like it. I only thought shrimping and rowing was hard work...plastering is a tough trade. But from a school chum I also learned to play the guitar and played in a band called the "Jesters." I liked the band in a way, but it had some serious shortcomings. Mostly we drank too much to keep the mood going and I finally became aware that the entertainment business was maybe the toughest profession of them all. After graduation and turning twenty-one we began to play nightclubs including the infamous "Porkey's."

I think the thing that saved me was a building recession that struck and the plastering trade took a beating and so did I. I tried to live off my guitar but that was a dead-end street. On top of it all the draft raised its ugly head. That did it. I was sick and broke and now about to get stuck in the military. I packed up and headed for home. I had a suitcase full of clothes and a guitar to show for my efforts. About the only dream left intact was the voyage.

I joined the army in the fall of 1961. Because of my mechanical knowledge I was sent to Ft. Rooker, Alabama for aircraft maintenance training. I did well in school, finishing in the upper ten percent of the class and went on to another more advanced school. I really wanted to work on helicopters, but at that crucial moment when the odd-numbered class went to rotor-wing school and the even-numbers went to fixed wing, they changed the rules. I was in the odd-numbers, but they sent me to a multi-engine school on the Dehavelin Caribou, a fixed wing aircraft. The only good thing about it was that I did get to fly on the airplane and was trained as flight engineer and as a private E2, drew flight pay. After graduation I received my orders to proceed to Ft. Dix, New Jersey and be sent overseas to Germany.

So, as fate would have it, I made my first transatlantic voyage on the troop-ship, William S. Darby. I was one of the few that didn't stay sick so they worked me in the kitchen and galley pretty hard. We landed in Bremmerhaven and took a train to Munich, then a bus to my duty station just North of the city on the small army airfield in Ober Schliesheim. True to form there was not a Dehavalin Caribou in Europe, and to top it off I was sent to a helicopter transportation company! Five months later I had a new MOS and was a crew chief on a Sikorsky H-34 helicopter.

I enjoyed the flying and in my spare time took my first stumbling steps to make my dream come true. One of our pilots had been a bomber navigator in WWII. While on standby duty one night in the hanger we started talking about celestial navigation. I knew that was one of the first hurdles I'd have to jump to make this voyage possible. Warrant Officer Wilson gave me a brief outline of how it was done and a list of equipment to get me started. It was really exciting and I was eager to get on with it.

First I needed a sextant. So I purchased an old army/navy bubble sextant. Next I ordered a copy of the current Nautical Almanac. For sight reduction tables, a copy of H.O. 214 covering my latitude, and to help me through it all, a hefty copy of Nathaniel Bowditch's "The American Practical Navigator." I also had purchased a Rolex wrist chronometer to mark the time. I was well armed with the essentials of celestial navigation.

After reading Bowditch and the Nautical Almanac concerning shooting the pole star for latitude, I took the sextant out one cold wintry night and after what seemed an eternity, I located and measured the altitude of that faintly glowing star.

Back in the warmth of the barracks I was greeted with hoots and good-natured ribbing from my buddies. They thought I was out of my mind. I managed a weak smile and made an honest effort to look very proficient over my formidable pile of publications. The barracks grew quiet. I felt the tension grow. I had to produce something tangible for the onlookers or suffer. They believed, as I had, that one had to be a mathematical wizard to navigate by the sun and stars. I worked on, putting in the necessary corrections to the sight and finally plotted the results on the chart. The resulting line went precisely through our position. I had accidentally made a perfect shot. I showed this to the hooters and they seemed satisfied. A few days later they were after me to show them how I did it, but I always managed to be too busy.

I was soon to learn that H.O. 214 was another bucket of worms altogether. It took the better part of one whole frustrating year to be able to get a position fix using the sun and then the moon and stars. But I could navigate and that was one major problem solved. The rest would be easy...I thought.

To buy a proper sea boat one needs money, but how much money? I didn't know, but a buddy and I were soon on leave and heading North to find out. Together we had accumulated $3,000 to buy our dreamboat. Everyone had told us how cheap the boats were in Scandinavia. We planned to buy one and after our hitch was over, sail her back to the States. We soon learned however, that was not the case. The boats we looked at, that were within our budget, were hardly suitable for an ocean voyage. We searched high and low, but it was of no use. Sea boats were expensive items to be had in any country. We went back to Munich down hearted and for the moment, defeated. The problem now switched to money, which had really been the biggest problem all along.

This called for some long-range planning. How does one with only mechanical skills and a high school education go about raising twenty or more thousand dollars? Well, I mused; unless a rich uncle dies and leaves it to you in his will, you'll have to work for it. It stands to reason that if you're going to work that long and that hard, you might just as well do something you're good at and enjoy doing. I decided to become a licensed aircraft mechanic. I would take the money I had saved for the boat and go to school and further my education in that field. I felt much better after making that decision and turned my attention to other things.

I still had almost a year to go with the army and rather than waste time I continued working with the sextant, improving my navigational skills. I also started reading numerous books about small boat sailors and voyages they had made. I was surprised at how many had gone to sea in small ships.

That last summer in Germany I managed to go sailing for the first time in a real sailboat. The army maintained an R&R center just South of Munich on the shores of beautiful Lake Chemsee. They had both Lightening and Star class sailboats and for a small fee they allowed military personnel to go out for half-day trips. This was a wonderful opportunity I could not and would not pass up.

I'll never forget how nervous I was the first time I set out in one of those trim little racing boats. My fears were groundless. The moment the sail filled and the boat began to move and answer the helm I knew that I could sail it anywhere. What a grand feeling to sail a real sailboat. I managed about twelve hours in the Star boats before heading back to the States and home.

I returned home to Daufuskie Island and began corresponding with several schools specializing in aircraft maintenance training. I was finally accepted at Northrop Institute of Technology in Inglewood, California. I considered it one of the finest schools available and was happy that I would be going there.

I spent the fall and winter of 1964 hunting and fishing with my father. During my absence my parents had opened a seafood restaurant on the Island called "Jolly Shores." The restaurant was very busy on weekends but slow during the week. So to offset the slack my mother became Postmaster for the Island and drove the school bus. My father in turn ran the mail to town by boat each day and was Magistrate Judge like his father had been. I gathered oysters for the weekend oyster roasts and trawled for shrimp and fish. School didn't start until the following spring.

And spring did arrive and the move to Los Angeles was made in a ten year old Chevrolet. It was beat up but other than for minor repairs, was in excellent mechanical condition. My younger brother, Gene, came along for the long drive West. Neither of us had ever been out there so we did the trip at a leisurely pace stopping along the way to enjoy the scenic spots. We thought the Grand Canyon was the most impressive. We also held up in Barstow, Arizona overnight so we could drive across the Mojave Desert in the heat of the day. It was a fascinating place and I still remember how the bread in our sandwiches turned crusty and hard like toast before we were done eating them. But the old Chevy ran like a clock and we finally arrived in San Francisco to visit our sister June before carrying on to LA. After a brief two days my brother headed home on a bus and I carried on to LA.

Upon arrival I found and rented an apartment close to school. In a very short time I decided that Los Angles was too big and too crowded for normal folks…but so what…I would probably be too busy to notice it anyway, and I was right.

I landed a job right away as an apprentice in a machine shop specializing in precision aircraft parts. I liked the work very much but the pay was low and I could barely make ends meet. I worked at that job for about three months. Then I learned that because of my military service and helicopter experience, I had met the time set by the

FAA that would enable me to take the written exams for my license. At the time I had completed less that a fourth of my schooling at Northrop. What had I to lose...nothing, and plenty to gain.

I took the exams and a short time later an envelope arrived from the FFA and I received the "airframe" portion of the two-part license. I had failed to pass one specialty on the power-plants part and would have to take it again at a later date.

With my chopper experience I lost no time in beating a path to the door of L.A. Airways, a helicopter airlines operating out of L.A. International Airport. They were in dire need of a line mechanic and hired me on the spot. I quit at the machine shop and looked forward to the higher pay at the airlines. I could have dropped out at Northrop, but I didn't want to do that, there was still so much to be learned in school so I stayed on.

Life became a sleepy blur for me. I worked grave-yard shift from eleven o'clock at night until 7 AM in the morning. School started at 7:45 and let out at 3:45 PM That gave me enough time to grab a bite to eat and hit the sack for a few hours sleep before starting all over again. My grades suffered but I still managed a "B" average. I studied when I could but mostly just paid attention in class. It was really tough but I hung on.

I came to realize that even with the new job I was still not making the kind of money I needed for a boat, nor would I ever. Living expenses were too high in L.A. I was getting discouraged and almost at a dead end when I got a break. I received a telegram, which read:

    IF YOU ARE INTERESTED IN A JOB OVERSEAS CALL AIR ASIA, INC. WASHINGTON, D.C. STOP.

The Dream Begins   15

I didn't stop but went immediately to a telephone and called them. After a short conversation about pay and certain tax advantages while working in a foreign country, I verbally agreed to a three-year contract with them. I would be stationed in the Far East, probably in Taiwan, they said.

School let out a week later and I loaded up my meager belongings in the old Chevrolet and drove back to the East Coast and home.

I spent a month there, fishing and relaxing and enjoying the slow pace. I caught up on my sleep too. Meanwhile Air Asia had arranged for me to take a flight physical, and get a series of immunization shots for such things as cholera, plague, yellow fever, just to mention a few. I also had to get a passport and send it to Washington. It came back a week later with a Taiwan visa and first class ticket to Taipei, Taiwan...my pay would start when I boarded the plane. They, who ever "they" were, certainly could get things done. It was some time later that I learned who "they" were. It was spelled C.I.A.

It's a long flight from Savannah, GA. to Taiwan. I was dog-tired when I arrived, but they had reserved a room for me in a first class hotel and the next morning a message was brought that told me to take a cab to a particular place and to check with a certain chap named Stubbs. I did as I was instructed and was ushered in to an office with pictures of airplanes on the walls. Stubbs was a big man, quite friendly, and he informed me that I was to be working in the Huey program. He also let drop that I really worked for Air America Inc. the fourth largest airline in the world. Funny I thought, "I'd never even heard of them."

What it all boiled down to was that Taipei was only a stop off to finish filling out paperwork before going on to my duty station and Air America. That would be in Saigon. *Saigon!* South Vietnam? Oh me! And I would be flying as a flight mechanic on Bell 204B helicopters! I reminded Stubbs that there was currently a war going on in South Vietnam.

"Oh," he said, glancing around at the pictures on the wall, "It's not so bad, we've got lots of people over there." "Yeah, right." I let it drop. No use getting fired now.

The next day I boarded an Air France flight for Saigon, but due to a crash on the runway and hostile fire we had to divert to Bangkok, until the situation cleared up. We spent about six hours in a hot stuffy terminal waiting for our flight to continue.

I struck up a friendship with a tech rep with Pratt & Whitney named Bill Kelly. He seemed to know the ropes and was a bit concerned about our delay. He explained about the 9 o'clock curfew in Saigon. And that it could be dangerous to be caught out after that hour. You could be legally shot on sight!

Finally our flight was called, but it was after curfew when we finally landed and had our baggage. Then we were crammed into an old, blue school bus that had seen better days and chugged off into the night, headed for downtown Saigon. Bill asked if anyone was going to meet me. I explained that I honestly didn't know. He told me not to worry about it…he had reservations at a hotel and would share with me. I really appreciated the offer.

There were troops and checkpoints everywhere. Concertina wire funneled traffic into to a narrow gap like a fish in a trap. But they just waved us on through and eventually we arrived at the hotel. The room had old, high ceilings and fans right out of a Bogart movie. There were two beds and the usual furnishings…I took a shower and turned in. I was very tired and dropped right off.

When I think of Saigon I think of loud explosions at night, heat, flies, yellow and blue taxicabs, Honda motorcycles and hopeless and endless traffic jams. There was constant harassment from the locals, the police and the bureaucratic officials. What it amounted to was constant squeeze for payoff. It was depressing and I never got used to it during the five years I spent in that country.

The next morning I called the company and they sent a van for me and we went out to Tan Son Nhut airfield. Boyd Messecher was my boss and put me in the paper mill. More shots too and a gate pass that I was to wear at all times.

Several of the pilots had leased villas and ran them as boarding houses. There was no problem getting a place to stay. Meals were provided, as was laundry. It was a bit better and safer than staying out on the economy. The flying portion of my existence was interesting to the extreme at times. Usually we hauled U.S. AID supplies to and from the various drop points and to hundreds of villages. We also moved U.S. Embassy officials and personnel from one place to another. At times these outposts would be under heavy fire from the North Vietnamese or Viet Cong, and then things would begin to get dangerous. It was what they called a dust-off operation. The Hueys were "slicks," that is to say, unarmed. We were called non-combatants and except for survival weapons, were unarmed. All this meant nothing to anyone. The bright, blue and white Air America helicopters made tempting targets and more than once we returned from a mission with bullet holes through the aircraft.

I had been flying for four months. War was hell indeed and I'd had enough. What good is money if you die before you can spend it! I had been a tech inspector for the last year of my army time and that made me eligible for a desk job in quality control. I jumped at it.

I was transferred up to Nha Trang...located on the shores of the South China Sea about half way up the coast between Saigon and Da Nang. I rented a house in a place called VC Village. It was a hotbed of infiltrators and was a real exciting neighborhood.

I enjoyed Nha Trang. It is considered the Ft. Lauderdale of S.E. Asia with lovely beaches and crystal clear waters. I even built a sailboard and honed my sailing skills. The nearby reef gave me opportunity to do some scuba diving and this helped break the gloom that was our constant companion. A war zone is a stressful place to live. Incoming and outgoing was not about the mail. Aircraft recoveries, test flights and tough working conditions kept the pressure on. Eventually I was transferred back into maintenance and after three years in Nha Trang moved back to Saigon.

No more beaches and scuba. I was an aircraft maintenance supervisor for the company. I enjoyed the challenge of managing about eighty Chinese, Vietnamese and Philippino mechanics, supervising the maintenance of about fifteen different types of aircraft, including choppers, and that was all I enjoyed. Rockets, terrorist attacks and traffic was a constant wear on nerves and body.

CHAPTER TWO
The Big Decisions...

The years passed and the money rolled in. My dream was close to becoming a reality and I started to search for my boat because by late 1969 I had solved two of the great problems standing between me, that boat, and making that long ocean voyage...

1. I had the money.
2. I knew how to navigate.

Now all I had to do was solve number 3; find the boat. I knew what I wanted and only had to find the boat that I had formed in my mind. After reading every book I could lay my hands on about small boat voyages and applying my own knowledge, I had gradually evolved the boat.

She had to meet five basic requirements, and they were:

1. She had to be between 28 and 32 feet in length.
2. She had to have a displacement type hull with a long, deep keel.

3. She had to have an outboard or lifeboat-type rudder (to simplify self-steering installation.)
4. She had to be sloop rigged.
5. She had to be of fiberglass construction.

There was my boat and all I had to do now was find her.

I took a month's leave from the company and armed with thirty days vacation, airplane tickets around the world and a fat checkbook, I caught a plane out of Saigon and went boat hunting. My first stop was Hong Kong and the Choey Lee shipyards. I liked the looks of the Bermuda 30 they built and was eager to take a first hand look at her.

I arrived in Hong Kong and checked into the Park Hotel. The next day I took a cab out to the Choey Lee yards...and got my first disappointment. After looking at the boat under construction and talking with the yard chief I decided against the boat. When I looked at her closely she didn't look like a tough enough sea boat for me. She was a very nice yacht but...and I really felt a pang of regret as I left Hong Kong and headed for the States and home for a few days.

The second boat on my list was the Sea Wind 30, built by the Allied Boat Company, a proven sea boat. Skippered by American Alan Eddy, she became the first fiberglass boat to circumnavigate the world.

Another disappointment. She was just too expensive for my budget. Prices the world over were on the rise. I went home and enjoyed a few days with my parents on Daufuskie Island before heading for England and the 1970 London boat show.

During my absence my parents had given up their seafood restaurant on the Island. My mother was still the

Postmaster and drove the school bus for the children going to school. My father had continued to trawl for shrimp with a small boat. He'd carry them to town with the mail and sold most of them in the post office. He was still the Magistrate on the island too. Island life really agreed with them because they both looked healthier and happier than I'd ever seen them. I enjoyed my short stay, but time was running out...taxes you know. I could go anywhere but home. I took a flight out of Savannah heading for London, England and the 1970 London Boat Show.

This brings us to the third boat I had in mind, an English boat, the Nicholson 32. Although she lacked the outboard rudder, I thought her a fine sea boat (and still do for that matter.) But after going over her at the boat show, I sadly found her a bit too expensive. If I bought her it would take all my funds and I'd have none left for spare equipment or the voyage back to the States. I kept walking and gawking at all the beautiful, expensive, lovely boats at the show. What was I going to do?

I gradually became aware of a little red sloop built in Denmark called the Great Dane 28. She had beautiful lines. Indeed, I finally couldn't keep my eyes off her. While she filled the five basic requirements for my dreamboat, she seemed small. I had previously seen an advertisement on the boat from a stateside firm handling her. She had been incredibly expensive. However she was a proven sea boat having been sailed across the Atlantic several times. Finally on the last day of the show I couldn't resist any longer and gave her a thorough going over. I was impressed. I had the chap at the booth work up a rough price with most of the optional equipment I wanted aboard. I was amazed at how much lower it was than the stateside price. But then I realized that the cost of shipping and import duty had been subtracted and it was a substantial sum. I was elated and went through the boat several more times. I liked her better each time. I became so excited that I hurriedly bought tickets for a side trip to Copenhagen to meet with the builder, Klaus Baess.

I caught a plane out of London that afternoon, arriving in Copenhagen after dark. The following morning I called Baess on the phone before going down to his office. I liked the man immediately and we got along just fine. He spoke excellent English. Not only did he have answers to everything I asked him, he produced photos of the actual tests being carried out on the boat. He would then produce a corresponding data sheet showing the graphs and charts of every question of strength that I came up with. I was most impressed.

I gave him a list of optional equipment. He quickly went through it with me, telling me if he could or could not supply the item. If not, how we could solve the problem. On most items he could fill the bill exactly. On the others he could give me the Danish equivalent. He also worked up a rough price on the boat and I was happy to see that it was close to the one the English chap had given me. I walked out of Baess' office two hours later with the knowledge that I would place an order on the boat as soon as we got all the extra equipment sorted out and a firm price established. I was happy with the decision and headed back to Saigon lighthearted and my head spinning over the rapid change of events. However, it would be almost four months and a letter per week before we had everything sorted out. At one point during negotiations I decided to ask him for a discount based on the fact that I was not going through a dealer. Surprisingly enough he gave me ten per cent right across the board. That amounted to about

$1,500.00. I turned around and put the money right back into the boat on extra equipment. It was a gamble that worked. Finally in May of 1970, I placed a firm order for one Great Dane 28, fiberglass sloop; color: blue.

Now the wheels really started to turn, but first things first. How about a name for the boat? I had given this more than a little thought and had come up with some possibilities: Sea Venture, Snark, Valkyrie and more, but none of them had the right sound or were right for the boat. I had to have a name that would say something of the boat and spell out her purpose. She would go places and she was blue in color, so it would be *Blue*...something. I thought for days on end and finally had it...she would be a wanderer, a Gypsy and every port would be home. I'd call her, "Blue Gypsy," but with a little different spelling, *Blue Gipsy*, with an "I," like the Brits, that was it! And it sounded good too. Next problem; should I have a crew or should I sail alone?

I had planned the whole venture as a solo affair. I really didn't want to ask anyone to go on the voyage; to have to depend on someone, anyone, who may back out at the last critical moment and leave me stranded. Still, I would like someone to go along. I kept quiet about that but talked freely about my plans to sail *Blue Gipsy* back to the States. I awaited developments.

They weren't long in coming. It seemed as if everyone wanted to go along. But did they? Not really. For the most part they just wanted to talk about it. A few days later they would be talking about doing something else. Meanwhile I collected gear and wrote letters to over one hundred manufacturers of marine and yachting equipment. I wanted to get the very best for *Blue Gipsy* and to make sure that it got to Copenhagen before the sailing date. That was the next item on the agenda.

When could I, or when should I sail? What would be the earliest time we could hope to sail from Copenhagen to avoid the ice on that end, and the hurricane season on the other end? I wrote to Baess and got back a rather vague reply. It would depend on:

1. How severe the winter was.
2. How thick the ice would get.
3. How early the spring thaw got underway.
4. Etc., etc...

What it boiled down to was, if they had a mild winter we could hope to get away by early April. If not it could be May or June. I decided that Denmark was going to have a very mild winter with an early spring, and that we would sail on the second of April, 1971. (No April fools here.) The hurricanes would just have to manage as best they could. I let Baess know my decision. He would have ample time to finish the boat and get her ready to launch the minute the ice was out of the harbour. He wrote back that he could see no problems if the weather cooperated.

The next big decision was where to make landfall on the other side of the Atlantic. After much thought I decided on San Salvador in the Bahamas. The same island Christopher Columbus saw on his epic voyage to the New World.

The next thing I knew, I had two crew members... one Harvey Kohler, a World War II bomber pilot and ex-schoonerman cum salmon fisherman from Marvel Bay, California. He was working with me in Saigon.

Ken Singleton was from Savannah, Georgia, a long time friend and hunting companion. This was great. It was decided that Harvey would sail from Copenhagen to

The Big Decisions 25

Falmouth, England with me where he would jump ship and continue his vacation. Ken would join me there for the remainder of the voyage. I felt that I knew both of these men very well. I knew that Harvey was a fine skipper and seaman. He had owned and operated his own tuna boat.

I had known Ken for over ten years and had fished and hunted with him on numerous occasions. Although he had almost no sailing experience he did know small powerboats and had served four years in the U.S. Coastguard. One very important asset that both men possessed was a solid sense of humor and neither of them seemed to be moody. Both were important points because of the weeks and months we would be together on the voyage. A happy coexistence was essential to the successful completion of the trip.

The pace became almost hectic as time ran out. My leave from the company started on March 14 and I planned to leave Saigon on that date. By the first of March I thought I would never make it. I started shipping equipment that had accumulated in Saigon, to Copenhagen via airmail. The cost was tremendous but I needed the gear, so had no choice. It was mostly charts and sailing directions. Ken also had a load to ship from Savannah, but he could utilize surface shipment at a greatly reduced rate. Suddenly Harvey had an emergency in his family and he had to leave immediately for the States and was out of the picture. This meant that Ken would have to join me in Copenhagen for the entire trip. No problem there. He was ready. I still had publications back ordered as time ran out. Some items of equipment were somewhere but not where they should be. Finally the day arrived when all that could be done from Saigon had been done. All that was left to do was to catch my flight out.

I breathed a deep sigh of relief when we lifted off

the runway at Tan Son Nhut airbase in Saigon. It had been a rat race with many problems. I had in a way, loved every minute of it. But it had become hectic and very stressful at the end. But here I was on my way to making my dreams come true.

The flight to Copenhagen seemed an eternity but my hopes for an early departure steadily sank out of sight... Rome: cold and cloudy. Frankfort: snowing and blowing. And at last Copenhagen: solid overcast with a light snow falling and lots of ice all around. I was very tired and fell into a pit of despair. I checked into a hotel in Kastrup feeling gloomy. After a meal and a couple of drinks I felt better so turned in for a good nights sleep. It seemed awfully quiet with no rockets coming in or small arms fire. It was great. I slept like a log.

The next day was Sunday when Ken flew in from the States and I cheered up immediately. It was good to see him and to have someone to talk to. We had plenty to talk about. Later in the day we took a walk down to the waterfront to see how the ice was doing. There wasn't any, At least not in the Sound. We continued walking and came upon a small yacht harbour and boat yard. Something about the place rang a bell in my mind. Baess had sent a photo of *Blue Gipsy* sitting in front of a building just like the one we were looking at! This had to be the yard that finished the boats for Baess. *Blue Gipsy* had to be here. A quick look around revealed two blue Great Dane 28s; one of them was *Blue Gipsy*. I couldn't tell which, so I took some pictures of them both. After getting over the excitement of finding her, we walked down to the railways where she would be launched. Was there too much ice?

There was indeed some ice but a chap with a long pike was breaking it up and pushing it out into the tide of the Sound. From the looks of it he would be done shortly and I could see no reason why we shouldn't be able to launch the ship on time. I whistled a cheery tune on the way back to the hotel.

The next day found Ken and I banging on the door to Baess' office. He was not there. He had suffered two broken Achilles' tendons in a skiing accident and would be out of action for some time. His able assistants knew about our situation though and would do everything they could to get us launched and on our way.

"Fine," I said, let's launch *Blue Gipsy*.

CHAPTER THREE
Blue Gipsy Readies for Sea...

It wasn't quite that easy of course. That afternoon we were at the yard when they moved *Blue Gipsy* into the shop to install all the extra equipment. Such as the Sum-Log, which would give us our speed and record the distance sailed, the self-steering, the cabin heater, the Sailor radio receiver with directional finding loop antenna, the bigger sailing grid compass, ship's clock and barometer, spare salt water pump for the galley sink, etc., etc.

Everything we tried to find a place for didn't want to fit. The little Taylor kerosene cabin heater just wouldn't fit anywhere. Then the sailing grid compass wouldn't fit in the binnacle. It was made to fit by removing the outer gimbals from the compass and shaving some wood from the recess in the binnacle itself, and then it fit quite well. That's the way things went the whole day.

Before we were through, the two-burner gas cooker with oven was packed up for shipment to the States. It was a very heavy stove with no gimbals. I didn't want LP gas in the boat anyway. The fittings to fill the bottles were different than ours in the States so it was best just to ship it home. A Primus two-burner kerosene cooker was installed in place of the gas range. "Lighten the ship," became the order of the day. Ken and I trudged back to the hotel exhausted, more mentally than physically. That night Ken came down with the flu.

The next morning dawned cold and gray. A light rain was falling and would probably turn to snow later. I set out walking to the yard alone. It would give me a chance to think. There were so many details that had to be dealt with. This was going to be serious business. The cold was a lot worse than I had envisioned. We'd have to be very careful. I decided to shoot for the 4th of April as a departure date. That would be my 32nd birthday.

I enjoyed the brisk walk but it was mid-morning before I arrived at the yard. It was my understanding that they were not going to launch the boat until the following day. I was somewhat aghast to see the double doors of the shop thrown open and a farm tractor standing by to haul the *Blue Gipsy* to the railways. They were in fact just short of launching her! I ran all the way back to the hotel and all but dragged Ken out of the bed. He couldn't miss this, even if he died of pneumonia later. When we got back they were moving her over the railway. There was no time to be sick. Just grab a camera and start shooting. I heard a commotion and looked around just in time to see Ken take a fall. He had stepped off the low sea wall to the icy ground and down he went, smacking the Nikonos camera on the wall as he tried to catch himself. I ran over hoping that he wasn't hurt. Luckily he wasn't, but the camera was a bit bent out of shape. Closer inspection revealed only the strap hinge broken and the light-filter bent. I could repair it, no problem. It was a real bulletproof camera. We kept shooting as *Blue Gipsy* slid down the ways.

In my journal I wrote in big block letters, "LAUNCHED"! It had taken me over ten years to get to this vital point in my life. I was very happy. It was the 18th of March.

With the boat in the water things seemed to calm down immediately, although it was probably me that calmed down. It looked as though we would have ample time to fit out before the April 4 sailing date I had decided upon. The following days found us busy as beavers moving all those boxes of stuff out of Basses' boat shed to *Blue Gipsy*. Then we had to find a place for it to live. Where was it all going to go? Somehow it kept disappearing into every nook and cranny.

The main post office and major ship chandleries were located in downtown Copenhagen. We would get a notice daily that there was a package to be picked up…or we'd have the need for a piece of hardware for the boat. Off we'd go in a cab. Not only was it time consuming but it was very expensive. It was burning up too much of my cash reserves, and something had to be done. It would be good if we could move the ship downtown. But that could be a problem…space was hard to come by in the canals of Copenhagen.

Enter Darryl and Birthe (pronounced Beer-Da) Bowles. He was American gone Danish and had married a beautiful, charming, blond-haired Danish girl. Both were avid boat nuts. I was wrestling with about six hundred feet of 3/4-inch poly anchor line that had to be stowed in the fo'c'sle when they walked up on the quay. Darryl said something like, "Somebody said that you guys are going to sail this thing back to the States."

"Yep," I replied, "If all goes as planned."

We introduced ourselves and after I finished up with the anchor line we adjourned to the local pub for a beer and more conversation. A warm friendship was quickly kindled between the four of us. We had dinner together almost every night. I would never have guessed how valuable these people would be to us in the days ahead.

Lancy Burn and H-34

Schliesheim Army Airfield

Air America Helicopter

DeHaviland Caribou (DH C-4 Caribou)

War at Night

C-47 Crash

Homemade sunfish

Heading for Copenhagen

Ice in Kastrup Harbour

Launching Blue Gipsy

Very Happy Man

Fitting Out

Darryl and Birthe

Little Mermaid

Downtown Copenhagen

Departing Copenhagen

Darryl was a seaman by trade and just happened to be working on a diver's boat that was tied up in downtown Copenhagen. I told him about our taxi problem and could he suggest any solution. Sure enough, there was enough room in front of the diver boat for *Blue Gipsy* to squeeze in. Not only that but he'd pilot us around whenever we got ready. Outstanding! We set a date to move the following weekend.

At this time we had not yet moved aboard or even been out for a sail trial. I wanted the ship loaded for that first time out. That way, she'd be new to us only once. There was no doubt in my mind that she would feel and handle differently with a half-ton of gear aboard. I wanted to get the feel of her ready for sea. We continued to load.

On the 26th of March we moved aboard, then in a rush decided to go sailing. Ken had brought a champagne bottle full of water to christen the ship with, but the launching had gone so quickly that we hadn't used it. He had found the bottle on the beach at Daufuskie and had half filled it with water from the river in front of my house there. Then he took the bottle to his home in Savannah to finish filling it from the river there. We poured the water over the bow of the boat. We didn't want to risk damage to the boat with a traditional christening. I cranked the engine and we motored out through the tiny entrance of Kastrup Harbor into the Sound.

It was a perfect afternoon for a sail. It was cold with a good strong breeze of 12-15 knots out of the north. *Blue Gipsy* proved to be a real sailing vessel, able to stand up to her canvas. I threw on every sail in the inventory at one time or another, including the big Genoa. We also gave the self-steering a good work out, but found it erratic, so we did most of the tiller work. We would wait until later to worry about the self-steering. That proved to be a grave error that would have a profound impact on us very soon. While we were sailing, all sorts of interesting loud crashing sounds were coming from the cabin. We were too excited and having too much fun to worry about that. All too soon it was over and with night coming on we returned to the little harbour at Kastrup. We were cold and wet but very happy with the way *Blue Gipsy* had performed. She was a honey of a boat. After tying up and securing the sails, we went below for a hot tea. What a sore sight it was that greeted our eyes. We had a lot to learn about stowing gear so it would stay put when the ship heeled.

With our new friends, Copenhagen became a different and exciting place. We were out on the town almost every night, eating and drinking until the wee hours of the morning. We enjoyed ourselves to the fullest with the fun loving Danes. As our circle of friends widened the pace became more of a test of endurance than anything else. We were gradually being worn down. Finally we came to our senses and I started pitching in the towel before mid-night and making my way back to the ship. Ken would usually follow, and as result we felt much better and accomplished more toward getting the ship and ourselves ready for the voyage. Time was running out.

The move downtown had proven a wise one and we accomplished twice as much in half the time and for a fraction of the cost. Most of the shops we frequented were right in the neighborhood. The weather was improving and we saw more sunny days. We were hoping for a pleasant trip South. Meanwhile, work on *Blue Gipsy* continued.

The fresh water system was giving me trouble. It was a real mess. For starters, you could only fill the main tank through the auxiliary tank. I wanted two completely separate water systems. I didn't want to risk losing all the water should one tank become contaminated, or develop a leak. I spent one entire, frustrating day going through the entire system and re-plumbing it as best I could. When I was finished, both tanks were separate. I installed a valve between them so I could drain the forward auxiliary tank into the main tank. The pump in the head and the one in the galley both drew from the main tank. Now each tank could be filled through its own through deck filler. I had wanted one pump coming off each tank but that would have involved cutting holes and welding. I had to compromise. It was still not what I wanted, but better than it had been.

All too soon our sailing day was upon us. One more day and it would all be over. Where had the time gone? Darryl had been keeping us up on the weather, since all the forecasts were in Danish. I was hoping that the weather would be fair for our departure, it would give us some much-needed time to adjust to the ship and its equipment. If I had only known…

CHAPTER FOUR
The End of the Beginning

Sailing day arrived, cold and wind-blown. I had planned to be away at daybreak but Darryl and Birthe, knowing our plans, showed up with a bottle of bubbly to toast us off and while she was there, Birthe decided to whip up a last breakfast for the crew. It was ten o'clock before we waved a last farewell and motored from the quay. We hated to leave all our newfound friends but we had to go. At ten thirty on the morning of the 4th of April we cleared the side entrance of Copenhagen Harbor.

We had five miles of visibility and light variable winds. The water temperature was 38 degrees Fahrenheit, and the air temperature was close to freezing. The sun was trying to burn through the haze. Maybe we would have a nice day. The forecast Darryl had given us called for force five winds; 17 to 21 knots out of the East and freshening. No alarms went off with that bit of news, so we set sail and were away at last.

An hour after clearing the harbour a good breeze came up from the East. I put up the large genny, hoisted the mains'l and shut down the engine...we were sailing well and were indeed off on the Long Voyage Home. Our itinerary called for two-days sail from Copenhagen to Kiel, Germany, hold up there for a day or so, then through the Kiel Canal to Brunsbuttel, Germany on the North Sea end of the Canal. Then depending on the weather, across the Elbe to Otterndorf. Ken's grandfather had migrated from Otterndorf to Savannah in 1888 and needless to say, Ken had quite a few relatives waiting for his arrival. After the reunion and a few days to see everyone, we would strike out into the North Sea for the English Channel and Falmouth, England. We would take on stores there before venturing out into the Atlantic and the Canary Islands. We would stop in Las Palmas for a few days to replenish stores and fix anything gone wrong with *Blue Gipsy* and from there on to San Salvador in the Bahamas and home.

Meanwhile, the fog was getting a little worse. The yellow orb of a sun never quite made the day. We had good sailing though, and the various buoys and beacons came up on schedule. We were making good time. Late in the evening I went below to get a radio fix of our position. I wanted to start navigating before everything was lost to sight. Visibility had dropped to less than three miles.

When I came on deck again an hour later, the wind had freshened and we were starting to sail hard. A short time later as the sun went down it started getting very cold. Darkness and more fog further reduced visibility. The wind was getting stronger and a sea was beginning to build. By 6 PM *Blue Gipsy* was hard pressed and it was time to reduce sail.

I struck the genny with thoughts of putting on the working jib, but by the time I had the genny down, in a bag and below, the wind was such that I decided on the little storm jib. The wind was force five (17-21) knots, and still coming. The seas were getting bigger. While putting on the storm jib our first wave broke aboard and wet me clear through to my bones. I carried on and cranked in four, full rolls of reefing in the main sail. There was a 20-lb. Danforth-type anchor in chocks on the foredeck with a coil of light line secured around it. It was our lunch hook. I started to put it below but I was so wet and cold I decided to leave it alone. It was tied down and would stay put. I hurried below for warm clothes.

By nightfall it looked as though a hurricane was upon us. The sea turned white with streaks of foam and the tops of the six-foot waves were getting blown off. Visibility was down to two-hundred yards. By now I had lowered the main sail completely and furled it around the boom. Even with the little storm jib we were making four knots in the right direction so we just hung on. Without the sun the air temperature dropped drastically. It was freezing and the wind had worked itself up to a force seven (28-33 knots) and was still increasing. We started getting some sleet and freezing rain mixed with snow. That really made things worse.

All the weather information was in Danish so I was not able to get an update. The first tinkling of alarm bells was going off in my head. I began to get the feeling that we were in for a hard time. Maybe we should turn the ship around and head back to Copenhagen. But honestly I just could not go back. We had finally got away and we'd carry on.

At this time we were off Stevens Klint, a point of rocky land jutting out into the Baltic Sea just South of Copenhagen. Ken and I were trying our best to keep warm and dry but it was impossible. The wave tops were beginning to break and *Blue Gipsy* was throwing up a lot of spray. Soon we were wet, cold and very miserable.

As the wind increased the waves grew higher and higher. Every few minutes we would hear a big one coming and have just enough time to bring the bow up to take it on the quarter. Otherwise we quickly learned, the sea would smash into the side of the ship and a solid sheet of near freezing water would be dumped right down in our laps.

Around midnight I went below and got busy on navigation. I needed a radio fix to determine how we were doing. It took a while because the motion below was quite lively and made any kind of work difficult. I finally came up with a good position and was surprised to see that we were being set into a large shallow bay behind the Island of Moen. I could see on the chart that the water shallowed well out from shore and I didn't want to get blown in there. The sailing directions warned about a strong current setting into the bay with an Easterly wind. That had to be the reason for our being pushed off course. Whatever the reason we had to tack and get out of there and soon!

I went out and gave Ken a break at the tiller. It was bitter cold and ice had started to form on the rigging. There was also more snow now but no rain. Ken went below to warm up, but was back very shortly. He was seasick. The motion below made him very nauseated. I let him steer and took one of our lightweight plastic space blankets and wrapped it around him, Hoping it would shed some of the spray and keep him warm. Then I made my way forward to raise the mains'l. We were getting pushed rapidly toward a lee shore and needed more sail up.

It was not easy getting to the mast. *Blue Gipsy* was really jumping in the ten-foot seas and there were patches of ice on the deck. I had to cling to every handhold to keep from being thrown into the sea. I had just started to unfurl the mains'l when I heard a noise up in the rigging...something was loose... clanging, banging around. I shined the flashlight up the mast and saw the spare jib halyard whipping around. It had gotten away and wrapped itself around the mast and rigging. There was nothing I could do about it, so carried on. I unfurled the main and started to raise it. It went up six feet and stuck solid! I grasped the flogging sailcloth and hauled down as hard as I could and nothing! It wouldn't budge either way...up or down. I heaved first on the halyard, then the sail but to no avail. The halyard had jammed at the masthead...probably from the runaway jib halyard. Disgustingly I furled the mains'l around the boom as best I could and went back to the cockpit. We were getting into a real jam. If we didn't come about soon we would run aground.

Ken was stiff from the cold and I wasn't much better. Our gloves and our clothes were soaked through. Each sea that boarded us drove the cold even deeper into our bodies. We had lost all feeling in our hands and feet. Fearing frostbite I took some plastic bags to cover our hands, they were the most exposed. It helped, but not much. Our teeth were chattering and waves of uncontrollable shivering would grip us. We were getting in bad shape. Something would have to be done and done soon, But what?

Meanwhile, we had still not come about and the depth sounder showed the water gradually shoaling. Ken had ducked below for a few minutes to warm up but I knew that he wouldn't be down long. He was terribly sick. We would tack the minute he popped up.

I sat at the helm peering into the inky blackness of that stormy night for any sign of land. Suddenly, there was something off to starboard. We passed a single piling! It stood stark, upright and evil in the milky water. The sight was electrifying. I yelled at the top of my lungs for Ken to get forward with a flashlight. We were running aground!

The End of the Beginning   39

He came out of the cabin fast and went immediately forward with the light. We were in a tight spot. While Ken trained the light forward I started the engine, jammed it in gear and made a 180-degree turn. Waves were breaking all around us and the depth sounder showed six feet. We drew five. By the time I got around there were more piling straight ahead. There was no time to do anything but aim between them. Praying that a third piling was not broken off below the water I drove *Blue Gipsy's* bow in the middle and held on. Just as the bow went through the opening, a huge cresting sea loomed out of the dark. Fearing the worst I shouted for Ken to hang on and held my breath. The bow shot up and up. I was surprised. I had expected *Blue Gipsy* to bury her nose and take it green over the top but the spunky little sloop showed her stuff and rose even higher. I could only think of a picture I had once seen of a Coast Guard lifeboat standing out through heavy surf on the Columbia River on the Pacific Coast...that is what *Blue Gipsy* must have looked like. The wave was breaking and we were right in the middle of it. She came down like an elevator almost undoing Ken. He had wrapped himself around the bow pulpit and jib stays. We cleared both piling and went on out through the shallows into deeper water. That had been close, too close, but we'd made it.

    I got well clear of the beach and then headed right into the teeth of the storm. There was deep clear water to the East of us. I handed the helm over to Ken and went below for another radio fix. No luck! With the engine running there was too much electrical interference from the generator. All that came through was constant static. I had failed to detect this during our sail trials. I asked Ken to shut the engine down so I could operate the radio.

    I flashed back to test flights in Viet Nam after an engine change on a single engine airplane. One part of the test called for a shutdown of the engine and a restart. It was always hard for me to reach over and hit that switch.

A half-hour later I got a rough fix that put us just off the tip of Moen. We had indeed been swept in behind the Island.

Shortly afterwards we sighted a buoy flashing in that dark and stormy night. I timed it with the stopwatch but had difficulty identifying it. My mind seemed numb and unable to comprehend how it all fit together...I finally sorted it out and felt reasonably sure of our position.

We were safe for the moment, but in order to clear the tip of Moen we would have to keep the engine running. I went out into the cockpit and pushed the starter button... nothing happened! I felt a stab of near panic. I jabbed the button again...still nothing. Ken said that the batteries were probably down from the running lights being on so long. I didn't think so. They were two very heavy-duty batteries and one of them was solely for the engine. Something else must be wrong...perhaps a faulty wire or connection. I had Ken throw the compression release levers on the engine and I tried again. Still nothing...we were sailing at four knots and I had an idea. I hit the starter again and jammed the shift lever into forward gear! thump...thump...thump! That sure sweet sound of the little diesel was music to our ears. We had a chance to clear the point. Maybe we could make it to Klintholm Havn; a small harbour on the north side of Moen. Dawn and the morning were still hours away.

At four in the morning we sighted a white light blinking through the mist and fog. I got the stopwatch and timed the flashes. It was the lighthouse on the very tip of Moen. We were, it seemed, going to clear the point.

I took the helm to give Ken a break, and suddenly a strange thing happened. I was convinced in my mind that the engine was going to quit. Just like that. I knew it without any doubt what-so-ever. I didn't ask any questions but called Ken out to take the tiller. I went below to rig our anchors.

The main anchor line was a 400-foot length of blue, 3/4-inch diameter polypropylene. Of the 600-foot reel that I had bought from Baess I could only get 400 in the locker. I'd given the rest to a yard worker. It was very light and incredibly strong. We had two lengths of 5/16 chains. One was 100 feet long, the other 20 feet.

We had three anchors aboard…two 20-pound Danforth-types and one 25 pound CQR plow. I attached the long piece of chain to the plastic line. On the end of that chain I shackled the 25-pound plow. To the back of it I shackled the short length of chain and on the very end the 20-pound Danforth-type that was below. The other was still up on deck. I felt that would anchor *Blue Gipsy* in anything should my intuition prove right. With that done, I went back to the cockpit and relieved Ken at the helm.

I was at the helm for perhaps five minutes when the engine abruptly stopped. Even though I had expected it I was still surprised by it. I let fly with a few choice words fit to warm up the North Pole. Was there no end to it? We were really in trouble now. Then I noticed that the depth sounder had quit working. Would nothing work? I missed that flickering red light that showed the depth of the water.

Next, the wind played its trump card; it shifted a little South of East. Instead of a beam wind we now had a quartering head wind. I pointed *Blue Gipsy's* slim bow up into the wind as far as I could and still make some headway. It was going to be a close call to clear the point with just 54 square feet of storm jib pulling us along. We got closer to the light. I kept it on my right and held my heading.

Earlier on, fearing that the batteries were indeed going down, I had turned off all running lights. But now I turned on the masthead light. This light cast a strong glow and in the coal black night lit up quite a large bubble around us. That's when I spotted the anchor line on the foredeck trailing over the side. It was bar taut. We had a rope in the wheel. The line coiled around the anchor on deck had gotten loose and was now wrapped around the propeller. How stupid of me! It was another bitter pill of failure.

Well, I thought, there was nothing I could do about it now so I just sat at the helm with eyes straining ahead... trying to see any threat of danger. The sight of those pilings earlier on haunted me.

The fog was back thicker than ever and I could no longer see the lighthouse flashing on Moen, but I could plainly hear the boom of surf off to my right, and it worried me as to what might lie ahead. Suddenly there were more piling...a whole cluster of them ahead and to seaward...and a thin line of them to shoreward...we were trapped! I was petrified for a second...not knowing what to do or where to turn. We had no engine or mains'l! I shouted to Ken to get on deck with the flashlight again, we were running aground. I switched on all the running lights. The seas were just forward of the beam now and breaking heavily. Ken couldn't find a flashlight in the jumble below. Ahead loomed a tight cluster of piling, dark and sinister. I aimed the bow of *Blue Gipsy* between the two that were widest apart holding as close as possible to the one on the left. A big wave smashed into *Blue Gipsy's* side, slewing her to leeward brushing the piling on the right. There was a bright flash of sparks as the green running light was wiped off the pulpit. The railing was unharmed. I shouted for Ken to forget the light and to come up and take the tiller. When he got there, I told him to turn towards shore at the first opportunity...there seemed to be less piling in that direction.

I dashed below and somehow heaved both anchors and the chain up through the forehatch and onto the deck.

The End of the Beginning 43

I held them there just long enough to see Ken, in the dim glow of the running lights, put the helm hard over. *Blue Gipsy* answered and her bow swung around smartly just missing two piling. I let the anchors go to starboard under the lifelines. The chain sounded like a machine gun firing as it peeled over the toe rail followed by the buzz saw sound of the plastic line zipping over the fore hatch coaming. It was snaking out so fast that I found it impossible to stop! There was no way I could belay it around the mast as I had planned. I shouted for Ken to, "head her up, head her up!" We were sailing very fast straight down wind. Ken put the helm over and *Blue Gipsy* swung up into the wind. I had to work very fast but my numb hands just didn't want to respond. I managed two turns around the foot of the mast and backed it up with two half hitches. *Blue Gipsy* had lost her momentum, she fell off broadside to the seas as a huge wave crashed into her side. As she fought to keep upright the anchor line snapped taut and snatched her around so fast it almost threw me off my feet. But luckily in the wild and dimly lit night I saw it coming and hung on for dear life.

The wave passed and I was able to pull the rest of the line from below. There was less than 20 feet left. That had been very, very close. The bitter end of the line was not fastened to anything below.

I had one more job to do…get the line into the chock at the bow rather than under the lifeline. As *Blue Gipsy* recovered and moved up on her anchors I untied the line from the mast and worked it from under the lifelines and then forward to the bow. I moved as fast as I could, I could see a wave coming. I worked frantically to get the line around the pulpit, through the chock and back to the mast. I tied off the bitter end at the very lowest part of the mast. *Blue Gipsy* had shot upwind quite a ways when that first wave struck but now she was drifting rapidly stern first, back down the line. She gained speed, but turned suddenly broadside to the wind and seas. I clung to the mast, knowing that I didn't have enough time to get back to the cockpit before the line came taut.

Blue Gipsy was coming down the back of a wave broadside when the anchor line caught her in mid-stride. She was snapped around like a roped calf in a calf roping contest at a rodeo. The motion was violent. I clung to the mast with all my strength and felt it tremble and shake. How long could it take that kind of strain? I didn't know. Somehow I didn't really care. The line sang again, and with a sickening splintering sound, the chock at the bow was ripped away, taking part of the toe rail with it. The stainless bow pulpit took the load and *Blue Gipsy* was hauled up sharply again. I worked my way carefully aft to the security of the cockpit. There was nothing more to be done so Ken and I retreated to the relative warmth of the cabin. We were exhausted, and the cold was numbing our minds. We kept quiet and rested.

The cabin was a wreck. The dinette table was smashed down. The Primus cooker complete with gimbals had been torn from the counter top and had joined the mound of books and gear on the cabin floor. What a mess. Everything it seemed was flung to the floor…including two drawers complete with contents dumped right on top. I salvaged the tabletop and made it into a double bunk. This gave us a somewhat comfortable place to semi-recline. By bracing our backs against the port side of the ship and our feet jammed against the counter on the other side we could stay put for a few minutes. We needed rest and hot food and drink, but there was no way that was going to happen in these conditions.

The motion inside the cabin was unreal. It was like some nightmare. The huge seas, cresting and breaking slammed into poor *Blue Gipsy* catching her awkwardly. Sometimes broadside, sometimes head on and even occasionally over the stern quarter. What made it so bad was the anchor line tied to the mast. Occasionally it would snap the ship over until the mast was almost flat on the water. The motion it created below was dangerous. We would brace our feet against the counter but as the ship was snatched around we would suddenly be wrenched loose and flung across the cabin. We were being slowly beaten to death.

Sometime later the first weak glow of a stormy dawn came sneaking over the wild scene. I went out to have a look at how *Blue Gipsy* was holding up against the onslaught. I was shocked at the sight that greeted my tired eyes.

With the anchor line tied off at the foot of the mast and nothing to restrain it, it had raised havoc with everything in its path. The bow pulpit on the starboard side was broken completely off and had disappeared over the side. The first lifeline stanchion was its next victim and followed in the wake of the pulpit. This allowed the line a free rein from the jib stay and stem fitting back to the chain plate for the forward-lower shroud. It had worn the toe rail down exposing the screw heads that held it on. They were fighting back, chewing pieces out of the plastic line as it grated back and forth. Something had to be done quickly. The line was in tatters and I wondered if I had enough time to shorten it before it parted.

As I made my way forward *Blue Gipsy* tried her best to pitch me off her tormented deck into the sea. I gained the mast, clung there until a large sea swept by, then as the ship ran up on the anchor line I took in about ten feet and made a fresh tie off at the mast. My hands had long ago lost all sensation or feeling and it took several attempts before I had the task completed. I was afraid that my hands were frozen but there was nothing I could do about it. I was thankful they worked as well as they did. I started for the cockpit but had an idea.

The bow cleat was made up of two heavy cast aluminum upright posts with a teak crossbar stuck through them. It looked fine but struck me as being weak. I had tried to get a suitable replacement; something more substantial to anchor a ten thousand-pound boat on, but nothing was to be found so it stayed where it was. Maybe it would come in handy after all.

I figured if I could throw a loop of the anchor line around the cleat that it might keep the line at the bow and not be destroyed by the jagged toerail. I worked my way forward until I was in a position to grab the line when it came my way. Finally I was able to catch it. It took every fiber of muscle in my tired body to place the line around that cleat… but I managed a single loop. Then I made my way back to the mast and clung to it to see what would happen.

A cresting wave came rushing in, *Blue Gipsy* rose to meet it and buried her bow in the foaming white top. The line became taut and sang when her weight came against it. With a report like a rifle shot the bow cleat was pinched off flush with the deck and disappeared straight up in the mist and fog, I didn't see where it landed. I made my way aft and went below. Tired, cold and dejected.

I made two more trips to the mast to shorten the chafing anchor line. On the second trip I saw that one of the two jib stays had been broken at the stem fitting and had wrapped itself around the mast top with the spare halyard. The other turnbuckle on the remaining jib stay was bent at a 45-degree angle. The fore hatch cover had been ripped from its hinges and was gone. By then I was numb to the very core and somehow didn't seem to care what happened. I went below exhausted and forlorn…my ship was being destroyed before my very eyes and I was afraid that the worst was yet to come.

My dreams had turned into a nightmare. A while later the fog briefly cleared allowing us to see for the first time the sight that greeted us astern. All our attention had been forward not aft. And the fog was so thick we couldn't see more than a hundred yards. It was grim and chilling in the cold gray light of morning. In my cold numbed mind I gave *Blue Gipsy* up for lost. I started thinking only of our survival...I knew that no ship could stand the test that waited behind us.

Only a few hundred yards astern there rose a cliff, white and sickly pale in the gray light of the stormy dawn. It seemed to rise straight out of the roaring, pounding sea. The top disappeared in the mist of swirling fog and snow. From my vantage point I could not see a beach of any kind, only rocks and piling and more rocks right up to its very base. Dark patches of spruce trees clung to its face. I wondered how high it went. I remembered the flashing of the lighthouse had been quite high. What difference did it make anyway? There was no way we could climb it in the shape we were in.

I racked my brain; was there anything I could do? Something I had overlooked, some way to snatch us out and away from all this? Suddenly I had an idea...maybe, just maybe there was a way. If I could get the line out of the propeller we just might be able to get the engine running and get out of there. It was a very slim chance. I would have to go over the side with a knife and cut the line out. Could I do it?

Looking back in my mind I had cut ropes out of the wheel of my father's shrimp boat. A grim business in the warm muddy, Carolina waters. But this would be far worse. I was weak from the long hours of battling for our lives, and numb to the core...even my mind didn't seem to work very well...it was dull and slow to think. The sea was also incredibly rough. But the water itself was the real threat. It was only six degrees above freezing. How long can a body function under those conditions? From what I'd read, only minutes. But it was our last chance and I had to make the effort. I had to play every card that was dealt. There would be no quitting in this game.

I had a wetsuit on board and told Ken what I was going to do. He said I was crazy. The water was too rough and too cold. I told him I had to give it a try. I rummaged around and found the wetsuit, mask, snorkel and fins. It took some doing to get them on and out into the cockpit but finally I was almost ready.

Ken went forward and shortened the anchor line. I took the filet knife from where it hung over the counter and went out into the cockpit. When Ken came back I went forward and cut off the excess anchor line that had accumulated as we had shortened it. I made my way back to the stern and sat with my feet hanging over the transom. Ken handed me a lifeline and I tied it around my waist. I was ready.

A wave swept through and as the ship settled down I grabbed the knife and dropped into the bottle green, ice-cold water. The shock was like a blow to my head. I saw lights flashing and it felt like my head was caught in a vice. I would not last long in these conditions. I took a deep breath and dove, grabbing the rudder to get me in close to the propeller.

Through the milky green water I could see that there was a big wad of line wrapped around the propeller blades. The lose ends were undulating in the water like the tentacles of an octopus. I took the knife and sawed at it…it was like cutting cable. The strain of the engine had turned the otherwise flexible nylon into something like iron. I ran out of breath and surfaced. I was fading fast. My body was being asked to do too much. I went back down and cut off some of the loose strands. It was tough going and I was out of breath again. I would not be able to get it all. I surfaced and threw the knife on the deck and Ken helped me aboard. I had to crawl below.

It took a while for me to recover enough to talk. It was a real letdown. I had not accomplished what I had set out to do. There was still some line on the prop. I wanted desperately to see if the engine would run and if the propeller would push us against the wind and sea. It was only five miles to Klintholm Havn. Ken went out and hit the starter...nothing. I released the compression levers...still nothing. Something else had to be wrong. Had the engine seized from lack of oil? I didn't know. I tried to move the flywheel by hand but it wouldn't budge. That did it. The ship was lost. We must turn our whole attention to survival.

I decided to talk things over with Ken and prepare for the worst. Our situation, even for survival, was getting slim. We were suffering from hypothermia and under these conditions it was only a matter of hours before we would freeze. We were still taking a beating from the wild gyrations of the ship and something had to give, something had to be done. We would take every action to survive.

First, we needed to shorten the anchor line one more time. We were both very weak from the cold. Ken was as sick as ever but said he'd go out and try. He was as bad off as I was. I tied the lifeline around his waist. He made his way forward and finally succeeded in shortening the anchor line. While he was gone, I contemplated our situation and came up with a feeble plan. It would not keep us off that deadly cliff, but at least it was something we would do.

When Ken returned he told me that a wave had

swept him overboard and in the same instant had scooped him back on board. I hadn't even felt a tug on the lifeline I held in my senseless hands. He was freezing and so was I.

While rummaging around for the wetsuit I happened upon the little emergency standby stove. I went forward, found it and lit the burner, burning my fingers in the process. I couldn't feel any pain but could smell the flesh burning. Maybe we could get a little warmth in our spirits if not our bodies. Both were in a sad state. The little stove roared merrily for about five minutes and sputtered out. The burner had clogged. Oh me! It was not funny. I was becoming bitter. I threw the disgusting thing forward out of sight.

Next, we still had the spare anchor on the foredeck. I went into the wrecked and dripping fo'c'sle. (The fore hatch was gone and a lot of water was coming in. I had noticed water over the cabin sole but compared to everything else it was nothing). By standing up through the fore hatch I managed to rig a 100-foot length of 3/4-inch braided nylon line to the anchor and put it over the side. I tied the end off to the stem fitting on the bow. I reasoned that when the main anchor line parted, this second anchor might slow us down and give us a few more moments to prepare for the eminent and terrible grounding.

Back in the cabin I suggested to Ken that we take all our money, passports, ship's papers and other valuables and place them in the sextant box. We would tie this to the spare five-gallon plastic jug of diesel oil and to it, the plastic container of alcohol priming fuel. We could also make up a waterproof bag with a lighter and matches. When the anchor line let go we would put the whole works over the side and let the oil and plastic containers carry the sextant box ashore. That way should the ship ground on rocks before reaching the cliff we would eventually end up in the water. Then if we got to shore we would be in crucial need of a hot fire. The diesel and alcohol would give us that even on a wet rock. The money would get us back to civilization. Ken agreed and we set about getting everything ready to go. We took time to shoot off all our distress flares too, hoping by chance that someone would see them from the lighthouse. Next we put our life jackets on and quietly waited for the anchor line to chafe through.

The flurry of activity warmed us slightly and the positive action taken for our survival seemed to ease our minds. We were both quite calm and thought that somehow we would survive. I felt strong enough to go out and shorten the anchor line one more time. I had also been toying with another idea of a way to keep the anchor line from destroying itself on that jagged rail.

We had some incredibly strong nylon webbing... parachute static line actually. If I could manage to lash the anchor line to the stem fitting, that may just save the day. It was apparent that the mast was standing the strain and the line was more than strong enough. The chaffing was destroying the line...

The trips out to shorten the line was destroying us. It allowed us no time to warm up and rest between trips. The beating we had taken below had not helped either. But it was the cold, bone-chilling, drenching that we got every trip to the foredeck that took the sap out of us. We needed warmth, rest and hot food. I decided to give my idea a try, why not?

I tied the lifeline around my waist, and just then the storm actually let up, but not much. I made my way as carefully and quickly as possible along the bucking deck to the mast. (For some reason, I didn't want to go out through the fore-hatch). It was pure torture. My hands refused to obey. It was maddening. I would almost get enough slack to make a turn on the mast when the ship would snatch it away from me. There was also a great wad of line built up on the mast from all the previous shortenings. There was no way to get it off. Finally after what seemed like hours I had it…but mashed my middle right finger in the process. It got caught between the line and the mast as a wave hit the ship. I didn't feel anything but I couldn't pull my finger out until the wave passed. My finger was flat. Blood oozed from around the fingernail. I studied it for a minute or two waiting for the pain but none came. It was beyond that.

 I made my way to the heaving battleground of the foredeck and clung to the jib stay and what was left of the pulpit. I had the webbing clenched between my teeth. A huge sea roared by and *Blue Gipsy* ran up on the line…but before I could get the webbing around the line and fitting, another sea swept in and took it away. This was repeated several times. I don't know how long it took but it seemed like forever. What torturous work, I was about to the end of my endurance. But at last the job was completed and seemed to be working. I was spent. Whatever happened now, would happen, I could physically do no more.

 I dropped through the forehatch, wondering why I hadn't come out that way. But then the lifeline caught me and Ken looked strange sitting there holding the other end and wondering what was happening. Then he saw me. I untied it from around my waist and he hauled it back. My mind was as numb as my body. I laid down exhausted and listened to the howl of the wind coming back and I could hardly believe my ears when it suddenly pitched a note higher than before. My grandfather's words came back to me, "When there's a lull in a storm, it's not about to quit. It's just reaching back for a better hold." He was right about that.

 The seas responded to the faster pace and got even

worse. It was incredible what *Blue Gipsy* was going through on the end of that anchor line. She was like a kite gone wild on a string. I knew that we would be heading for shore soon and rested as best I could. We would both need all the strength we could muster for the coming ordeal. We waited in silence.

There was no fear between us, None visibly anyway. Were we too exhausted, too far-gone to really appreciate our position and to comprehend the full impact of the situation? I don't know but I don't think so. I think that we knew the situation as it was and accepted the fact that we were going ashore and the preparations gave us the assurance that we would somehow survive. Even the conversation we'd had about getting ready for the grounding helped calm our minds. There was hope and that calmed fear. We were very concerned, however about the fate of the ship and for each other. The one thing that bothered me was the prospect of spending another five years in Vietnam for another boat. I just couldn't do it again.

Suddenly a great wave came roaring in. We could hear it above the screech of the wind and braced ourselves. *Blue Gipsy* was broadside to the sea and I knew that this would probably be our ticket to shore…It was! The gallant little *Gipsy* was game, but the anchor and line wouldn't give her the freedom she needed to ride over and through a sea such as this. She rose bravely to the challenge side ways, raising higher as the sea came on. The roar of that huge breaking crest was deafening as it crashed down on the boat with a ferocity that I have never seen or experienced before. All I saw through the windows was green water. Water gushed in everywhere. We were both flung across the cabin. The anchor line come taut and then with a sound like a cannon shot, it parted! Free of her anchors at last, *Blue Gipsy* righted herself and rode quietly on the rough seas. She seemed almost happy to be free. We had little time because we were drifting rapidly toward our next test, the rocky shore of Ichlishound, Moen Island, Denmark.

Ken and I both knew the line had parted and set about getting the sextant box and plastic containers out into the cockpit. I expected to see the mast torn out of the ship but it was still there. The noise and crashing had been terrific. The third anchor I noticed was having little or no effect on our drift to shore. We put the sextant box over the side with the containers of fuel and the bag of gear. I took the tiller and tried to steer *Blue Gipsy*, stern first, to shore.

I wanted to keep her bow to the seas and present the smallest possible target to the black rocks that were waiting to rip her to shreds.

I tried, but she would fall off as the wind blew her bow around. Then the waves would come thundering in, smashing into her, slewing her bow around down wind and she'd pick up speed and I'd bring her back up. At first I thought the breaking waves would roll us right over but they didn't. I felt a swell of pride as I watched how she would rise to the wave, then roll to leeward sharply as the crest smashed into her, and then she would actually surf down the face of the wave at an angle of 45-50 degrees. I gained tremendous respect for her show of absolute sea worthiness.

How sad, I thought, that she would never get a fair test in a real ocean.

As we approached shore my hopes for survival soared....there was a beach! Only a small, narrow, wave swept rocky strip, but it was a beach! Ken and I gripped a life ring between us and agreed to stay together if at all possible. Also, stay with the ship! Leave only when safely ashore or washed out of her. She would offer better protection to us than floundering around in the freezing surf. We struck! The tiller slammed into my left side pinning me momentarily to the side of the cockpit. It knocked the breath out of me. It felt like something broke but it was the tiller. The screws had pulled out of the cheek piece on one side. The rudder must have hit a rock. *Blue Gipsy* vibrated from one end to the other from the blow...another wave came crashing in and smashed into her side, laying her far over and pushing her off the rocks. She was free, but only to come up with a bone jarring impact against another. This impact was not as severe as the first. This was repeated several more times until we reached the rocky strip of beach. Then a huge wave roared in and smashed into *Blue Gipsy's* side, throwing her bodily on the beach. I told Ken to jump ashore and I'd pass out some gear. Our sleeping bags first, then the stove and food. We would need these should the waves drag *Blue Gipsy* back to sea and swamp her.

It took only a couple of minutes to do this and as I worked I noticed that the motion of the boat had all but ceased. Only the biggest waves caused her to move at all and these only nudged her further up on the beach. I yelled for Ken to come back aboard. He did and we just sat quietly in the cabin and rested for a moment and waited to see what *Blue Gipsy* would do. It was soon evident that she was hard aground. Ken made his way back to the beach, passed our gear aboard and for the moment we were safe, now what...?

CHAPTER FIVE

How Do You Salvage a Dream? Very Carefully...

With *Blue Gipsy* hard aground, Ken and I both breathed a sigh of relief hoping that the worst of our ordeal was over. The next item in order was to get warm. We were in very bad shape from the cold...we also needed to get some hot food into our empty stomachs.

It took some doing to dig the Primus cooker from the pile of gear that Ken had handed back aboard. Then we had to find all its small parts, put fuel in it and get it going. My hands had no feeling whatsoever. I had to watch every action to make them work. I fumbled and dropped things. I had to be careful not to use my smashed finger. It was like trying to do a job with clumsy, mechanical hands. I had to work by sight, not touch. But they did work and I finally had the little cooker roaring at full blast with a big pot of tinned beef stew heating on top.

As that warming glow from the cooker spread through the cabin, we began to feel the wonderful heat. But suddenly excruciating pain spread through our hands and feet! They had been on the brink of freezing for so long the circulation must have stopped. They also began to bleed...every little cut started seeping blood. That's when we noticed for the first time what a beating our hands had taken.

It took some doing to locate the medical kit in the chaos inside the ship but we found it and started patching each other up as best we could. Ken's hands were badly beat up with small cuts and bruises but nothing serious. Mine were somewhat worse, especially the ring and middle fingers on my right hand. The anchor line had pinned them against the mast and mashed the ends. The middle one appeared to be broken just below the end joint. Since we had to wear gloves I decided not to put a splint on it. I put a Band-Aid on it and pulled my glove on for support. With that out of the way, we sat down to our first hot meal in over thirty hours.

After eating we felt much better and our spirits soared. It was good to be alive and we still had the ship. We started to clear up the mess below. Ken went forward and nailed a sail bag over the forehatch to keep any more water from coming below. I picked up and tried to sort out the cabin. I just tossed most of the items into the fo'c'sle. We would deal with drying it all out later.

We had come ashore about 10 o'clock in the morning and by the time we had accomplished the first aid, had a meal and sorted through our wet gear it was late afternoon. The storm still raged outside and as the warmth penetrated our bodies we became very tired and sleepy. There was nothing to gain by staying up so decided to turn in and try to get some much needed rest and sleep.

I laid my sleeping bag out along the counter tops and cabinets. *Blue Gipsy* was heeled 45 degrees to starboard so I didn't have any trouble staying put...cushions filled in the sharp angle between and I was quite comfortable. Ken had the quarter berth and even in our wet sleeping bags, we were quite warm and snug. We dropped off to sleep immediately.

I awoke several times during the night when an extra large wave would nudge *Blue Gipsy* higher yet onto the rocky beach. Or from the noise of rocks being hurled against the hull. There was no doubt that the storm was still out there.

The next morning, I awoke with a start, confused, and not knowing where I was. Then I remembered the events of the previous day and our grounding. I relaxed and listened to the storm, the moaning wind in the rigging and the waves crashing ashore on and around the hull of *Blue Gipsy*. It was bitter cold outside and it felt good to be warm and cozy in my sleeping bag. Ken was still asleep. I lay there and tried to think. We were still in one heck of a mess. How were we going to get *Blue Gipsy* back in the water? We needed to be on our way as soon as possible. Time was of the essence because if another storm like this one came through *Blue Gipsy* would surely be ground to pieces on this cold and rock-strewn beach. We needed a plan of action, something to work on. We would need help too, and perhaps some equipment, but first things first. How badly was she damaged? There seemed to be a lot of water in the bilges. Was this from the missing hatch cover? Maybe and maybe not, it was hard to tell.

Logically the first thing we must do was to assay the damage, and from that work up a list of materials we'd need to make temporary repairs. Then we could limp back to Copenhagen for proper repairs.

But the biggest problem of all was how we were going to move her off the beach and back into the water. That was going to be an enormous task.

Satisfied with my thoughts, I tried to get up. Every muscle and bone had its own sharp pain. I felt like I had been hit and run over several times by a very large truck.

My hands were awful. It was impossible to clench them. The middle finger on my right hand was fat and blue from the tip back to the middle. The ring finger next to it was almost as bad. I could see no sign of burns or frost bite and I was happy about that. Bones can mend, but a bad case of frostbite would be something else entirely. My left side was extremely sore and tender where the tiller had caught me. I could detect nothing broken. Hopefully it was just a bad bruise. We were very, very lucky to be alive and all things considered, we had gotten off lightly.

I finally managed to get up. Moving slowly and painfully, I lit the Primus and got breakfast started. We had slept for sixteen hours.

MY JOURNAL, April 6, 1971...

"The waves are still hitting Blue Gipsy hard, but not like they were. The storm is beginning to let up, albeit slightly. The barometer is still reading a low 1006 millibars. I hope it lets up soon so we can get to work...we must get Blue Gipsy *back into the water."*

Ken got up and while I cooked breakfast, he tried to sort out the pile of wet, soggy gear forward but it was a hopeless mess and he gave up and went outside. A little while later he returned with the sextant box and our valuables. What a stroke of luck that was! We chucked it forward with the rest of the stuff and we sat down as best we could to breakfast.

With the ship heeled 45 degrees it was very difficult to move around inside, cook, or just sit. The toilet was a real challenge. Since it was on the high side of the ship. We lined the bowl with a plastic trash bag and would cart that off after use. It was a lot better than braving the windy spray-swept beach.

The wind continued to drop while we ate and by the time the dishes were cleared away it was down by half of what it had been. We wasted no time in getting out and making a list of the damages...

1. One half of the bow pulpit had torn away.
2. Ten feet of the starboard toe rail torn off, exposing the bolt heads.
3. Forehatch cover ripped off its hinges and missing.
4. Bow cleat sheared off, and gone.
5. Port jib stay broken through the turnbuckle.
6. Starboard jib stay turnbuckle bent 45 degrees.
7. Mainsail slot at the foot of the mast squeezed shut.
8. One halyard cleat torn off the mast.
9. Servo tab on the self-steering bent 20 degrees.
10. Spare jib halyard jammed in the main halyard sheave at the mast top.
11. One 6 inch crack in the starboard side of the hull, just below the turn of the bilge and seeping water.
12. Rudderhead split two feet down the back.
13. Screws pulled out of tiller cheek plates.
14. Lower rudder gudgeon pulled out of the hull.
15. Numerous items of small gear broken or damaged, Including dishes.
16. Last, but not least, the engine was seized up, and wouldn't turn over.

We started clearing up the deck and further checking for damage. I walked up the mast like a Polynesian up a coconut tree and cleared the main and jib halyards. I also retrieved the jib stay. We put new turnbuckles on the twin head stays and furled the main sail. By lunchtime, *Blue Gipsy* was looking more like a grounded sloop than a wrecked one. It was also good news that most of our damage was superficial. The fracture through the hull was an exception, and would have to be fixed before venturing out to sea.

After lunch, while Ken continued the clean up operation I decided to go for help. We had already walked a few hundred yards North along the beach until we were below the light and saw that it was a mechanical light with no keeper. This time I turned South and set out along the beach.

I was wearing short rubber deck boots and it was rough going. The slippery, wet stones, anywhere from pebbles to basketball-size, were very difficult to walk on having been worn smooth and round by the pounding surf. A half-mile from the boat I found remnants of an old stairway leading up a break in the muddy clay of the cliff. It was rotten so I very carefully picked my way upward. In a short while I cleared the rim, and found a road a stones-throw back from the edge of the cliff. I followed it South passing a deserted house along the way. Another half-mile brought me to the edge of a vast green lawn. There were several ponds down the middle. Swans and ducks were paddling about.

I thought at first that it was a golf course. I ventured a bit further. I was amazed to see off to my right, a low sweeping hill, and on top facing the sea stood a huge and elegant mansion. It was picture-postcard perfect, an oasis of greenery, tranquility and beauty. What a contrast to what we had been through. Then I couldn't help but wonder if I had not accidentally stumbled onto the King's summerhouse.

I abandoned the road for a gravel path that led to the rear of the mansion. I met a group of students who informed me that this was the estate of the Baron Von Rosenkruntz. It had been turned into a park. Students used the mansion itself as a place to study. They told me that the Baron lived in the next house up the road. I thanked them and went to see the Baron.

The Baron's house was built around a square courtyard. In days gone by it must have been the servant's quarters. There were stables in one end and shops along the sides. The Baron answered my knock and I liked him instantly. He was in his mid fifties, with graying hair and a neat mustache. He had a warm and friendly smile and spoke excellent English.

I learned that he was a retired colonel in the Danish Calvary and that he was in fact, a true Baron. He told me how times had changed. Taxes and operational costs had gotten to be exorbitant. Finally he turned the estate over to the Danish Government but with special concessions allowing him to remain on the property.

Then the conversation turned to me. He patiently listened to my story, amazed at what we had gone through. He said that the storm had been one of the worst of the winter. Being a military man he came right to the point and asked what he could do to help us. I explained that I needed to contact Baess and let him know what had happened. I was hoping that he could get a rescue team together and help us get off the beach. The Baron quickly explained that any help would have to come via the sea. There was no road access down to the beach where *Blue Gipsy* lay. That changed any thoughts. In my mind, I had a mobile crane lifting *Blue Gipsy* back into deep water.

Meanwhile the Baron got busy on the phone, but was unable to contact Baess. The Easter holidays were in full swing and everything was shut down for at least a week. I had him try to contact Darryl. No luck, he wasn't home. I didn't know what to do. Finally I asked the Baron if he would try later to contact Baess or Darryl and tell them what had happened. Hopefully one of them could get us the list of items I needed to start moving *Blue Gipsy* off the beach. The list I gave him was:

1. 1 - 20mm diameter rope, 300 feet long.
2. 1 - fisherman type anchor, any size.
3. 1 - snatch block for the size rope obtained.
4. 1 - square yard of fiberglass cloth
5. 1 - quart of polyester resin with hardener.

    I also needed some hand tools but the Baron assured me that he had plenty and would be more than happy to lend them to me. With nothing further to be done he led me out to the shops. I picked out two short-handled shovels, an axe, a bow saw, a hammer and a box of large square nails. The Baron insisted on helping me carry all this back to the ship. I happily consented because it was quite a load. Apparently he wanted to take a close look at what had washed up on his beach.
    There was a new stairway leading down to the beach in front of the mansion. This made getting down much easier. When the Baron saw *Blue Gipsy* he was very sympathetic. He warned us that storms were frequent this time of year and that we must do everything within our power to get the ship back in the water as soon as possible. Another such storm and *Blue Gipsy* would be totally destroyed.
    That was exactly my line of thought. I also had the feeling that if we were going to save *Blue Gipsy* we had

better get on with the job. Help may be slow in coming, if it came at all. Half an hour later the Baron bid us goodbye, saying that if we needed anything at all to let him know and he would help us all that he could.

Our spirits rose with that bit of assurance. How good it was to have someone on our side in time of need! I even became a little optimistic and felt that help would really be on the way once Baess got the news of our plight. It was too late to do any work so we stowed our tools and got busy inside the ship, trying to make life as comfortable as possible in a world tilted 45 degrees to starboard.

That night I lay in my sleeping bag turning the events of the day over in my mind. My optimism dropped. I somehow realized that we could not rely on receiving help from the outside. I could not afford monetarily or justify letting someone else take the responsibility of getting us out of our predicament. We must form our own plans and use whatever means available to get the ship back in the water. If help does arrive, fine, direct it where it is most needed and carry on.

Actually we had a lot going for us...such as tools from the Baron. There was an unlimited supply of timber along the beach. I had noticed this, and asked the Baron about it. He said that the timber was too heavy to carry up the cliff, so no one bothered with it. There were boards and lumber of every description along the rocky shore. It was ours for the taking. Also, with the seas moderating and with any luck we could probably retrieve our anchors and line. I also had enough block and tackle on board to give us the necessary pulling power to move *Blue Gipsy*. If my grandfather and I could move that heavy old bateau off a muddy shore alone, I mused, and if the Vikings could move their long ships overland using rollers, then Ken and I should be able to move *Blue Gipsy* fifty feet to the water. With that decision made, it was only a matter of formulating a plan of action and getting busy. I finally dropped off to sleep with all sorts of ideas racing through my head.

The 7th of April dawned cold, gray and foggy. The wind had gone down during the night leaving only a gentle sea washing ashore. After breakfast, I got the rubber Avon dinghy blown up and launched. I was soon rowing among the piling looking for my anchors. The Baron told me that the fishermen put the piles up to hang nets on to catch fish and eels during the warm summer months. Suddenly I saw a flash of blue close to one of the piling and sure enough, it was my anchor line. It floated!

I quickly started taking it in. It was a tiring job because the line had wrapped itself around every pole and rock. An hour later I had it, anchors and all safely in the dinghy, but Not without a price, I had reopened some of the wounds on my hands. The smashed fingers were bleeding and very painful, but I had my anchors! Mission accomplished! I was elated.

The next thing was to right *Blue Gipsy*; get her on an even keel. Ken and I unshipped the rudder to keep it from receiving further damage and went about setting the anchors. I rowed the dinghy straight out from shore and put the anchors over as far as the line permitted. Next I took the mainsheet tackle, a double fiddle block, and tied one end into the anchor line and the other end to the main halyard. I ran this up the mast and hauled it as taut as possible. Then by putting the tail of the sheet around the jib halyard winch we could exert enormous pulling power on one great lever, the mast.

Everything was ready. We started winching on the tackle. The pressure built up but just as *Blue Gipsy* started to move the anchors pulled out, and she settled back down. We shortened up on the anchor line and tried again, but again the anchors pulled out. They just couldn't get a good grip on the rocky bottom. We heard someone shouting and looked up the beach to see Darryl and Birthe struggling along under a huge load of gear.

We dropped everything and ran to help, we were very happy to see them. In addition to a heavy coil of rope, they had a steel snatch block that must have weighed twenty-five pounds, plus a package of food and a case of good Danish beer! It's amazing how they managed to lug all this down the cliff and along a half mile of rocky beach. We were all very tired from our work and so we stopped for lunch.

While we were eating, I filled Darryl in on our plans. (He confessed later that he really didn't believe that we would ever move the boat). He added some helpful hints of his own and when the meal was over, we got back to work.

Birthe stayed inside the ship and began really cleaning up as only a woman can. The rest of us went outside to work. First, Darryl and I rowed out in the dinghy to reset the anchors. Instead of running the anchor line straight out from the ship Darryl suggested that we lay the line straight until we got to the chain portion, then turn 90 degrees and run parallel to the beach. The theory being that the chain would become lodged behind a rock and help the anchors to take the strain.

We rigged the tackle to the mast again and started winching, and the anchors held. As *Blue Gipsy* started coming up, the mast began to bend! It had not been designed to take that kind of strain. Darryl was very concerned about this but all I could say was; "If it breaks or something pulls loose, we'll just have to so something else. Keep winching!" Things went smoothly and in a surprisingly short time *Blue Gipsy* was upright and on even keel. We set four posts as deep as possible into the rocky beach, then nailed bracing between them to hold the ship upright. We also left the anchors set. Should a strong wind come up during the night they would help steady her. It would be a sad and rude awakening if the ship blew over. With *Blue Gipsy* upright the damage to the hull could be easily inspected. We were all very happy to see that most of the damage was to the gel coat. There was however one small, horseshoe-shaped crack on the starboard side amidships and just below the turn of the bilge. It went through the hull. Darryl said that he would bring some fiberglass cloth and resin the next day to repair it. It would need to be completely cured by the time we were ready to launch, whenever that would be.

    That afternoon in the midst of shoveling stones from around the keel of *Blue Gipsy*, a man came up and started talking to Darryl in Danish. He was carrying a six-pack of fancy, foil wrapped, bottled beer. After a short conversation Darryl turned and said, "Bob, this guy is from Baess' office and he says that because of the Easter holidays, they can't get any of that stuff you wanted." The news was a disappointment to me. He handed me the beer. I guess it was to wash down the bitter news. I passed it around and we drank it up on the spot...the messenger helping.

    So there it was..."If you want the ship off the beach, you'd better get busy," was the message I really received. There would be no help from Baess' office in Copenhagen. I thanked the man, and he left us.

    That evening, after Darryl and Birthe left, we had more visitors, Sevend Jorgensen and his young son Lars. They had come to see the wreck everybody was talking about. They both spoke very good English and invited us to their farm for a home cooked meal and a hot bath. We gratefully accepted their invitation. We then showed them around the ship. It was decided that Ken would go the next evening and I would go the following day. I didn't want to leave *Blue Gipsy* unattended. We enjoyed having them visit. It was almost dark when they left.

Ken and I put our tools away and called it a day. We were both very tired. I cooked supper. After we had finished eating Ken went out to wash the dishes. I started getting a plan together to move *Blue Gipsy* back into the water.

We would have to build some sort of a cradle or carriage to put under the ship. This would give us a strong platform to work with, without doing more damage to *Blue Gipsy's* battered hull. Then we would have to clear a level area, a fairway of sorts to the waters edge; now some twenty feet away. This fairway would have to be planked with heavy boards. We could use small spruce trees for rollers like the Vikings used. The carriage under *Blue Gipsy* would roll along on these. Ken came back in and we talked over these ideas. Then more talk and more ideas. Finally we had a plan that went something like this:

1. Level the rocks from the water's edge back to the ship's keel.
2. Use some of the heaviest boards lying along the beach as cross ties. Over these lay boards edge to edge, making a stage or ramp out into the water as far as we could go.
3. Cut small spruce trees, (mud slides brought many of these down the cliff), 3 inches in diameter, 8 feet long as rollers.
4. Build a three log, travis-type carriage with the logs fanning out to support the ship's keel, forward, center and aft. This would be assembled on the rollers and under the ship's keel.
5. When all was ready, we would get a local trawler to drag the whole thing off the beach.

This all sounded simple enough and gave us a positive plan from which to work. We felt much better and more confident about getting *Blue Gipsy* afloat.

The next morning, April 8th, was our third day on the beach. Darryl and Birthe arrived with the fiberglass and resin. I was very familiar with the material from patching up our boats back home. I simply put scab patches over the worst looking places. Only that one had penetrated the hull.

While I worked, I came up with the thought that we may not go back to Copenhagen for repairs at all. Baess had not been very helpful. Why not carry on to England for repairs? Copenhagen just didn't seem like the place to go; too many parties, too many distractions and very expensive. The money was flying away. I had to be careful. I kept my thoughts to myself and didn't mention this to anyone. We would sort that out after we were afloat.

After I finished with the patches, I started helping Ken and Darryl. There were tons of stones to be moved. We used the shovels and pick I had borrowed from the Baron. Darryl also had borrowed a small hydraulic jack from a chap with a truck. We used it to jack the ship straight up high enough to get the staging, the rollers and the carriage under the keel. This was slow, cold and tedious work. The smooth round rocks were not the most stable medium to set a jack on, but by using large blocks of wood under the hull and making a pyramid of blocks on the stony beach, it worked. We'd jack up the bow six inches and then the stern, all the while adjusting the braces and props that kept the ship from toppling over.

Next we began collecting materials for the stage, logs for the carriage and trees for the rollers. By the time Darryl and Birthe had to leave we had things pretty well roughed out.

Sevend and Lars arrived and were surprised at the progress. Ken got his kit together and they trudged off up the beach, leaving me alone. The cold fog rolled in and I put our tools away and went inside the ship. I got the cooker fired up and soon it was warm and cozy. I heated canned stuff for a meal. After eating and washing up, I decided to go over our plans and refine them where possible. We had collected some of the materials, and located the rest. We needed only to get them to the site and assemble the various parts of the stage and cradle. It sounded so easy. But I knew better. This was going to be some of the hardest, most painful work we'd ever done. We had hardly gotten started and our feet were already sore and tender from walking on the cold slippery rocks. I tried not to think about the misery of the next few days. We still had plenty of walking to do.

Ken returned just after dark and we sat down and talked over the plans I'd sketched out in crude line drawings of the stage and the carriage. He thought that it would work all right. Then we started talking about what we would do once we got afloat. I broached the subject of going on to England for repairs. Ken pointed out that we really should go back to Copenhagen, at least to get the engine repaired. That was a good point, even if we afterwards decided to go to England for repairs to the hull. Then Ken had a sound suggestion...why not let the people who built the boat, repair it? They should know better than anyone else how it should be done. I couldn't argue with the logic of that, although I didn't feel that it would necessarily work out that way.

During the conversation we speculated as to the cause of the engine quitting, lack of oil from the boat heeling too much? The oil drained out through a broken line or the like? We decided to have a look. I took the top of the engine box off and tried to remove the front, but it seemed to be stuck. I got a flashlight and discovered that the flywheel was pressed hard against the side of the engine box. The engine must have shifted. I forced the front off and checked the engine mounts and they were fine. With the front of the motor box removed the flywheel turned freely! I jabbed the starter button and the engine fired right up. What an enormous relief that was. There was nothing wrong with the engine. That was one great problem solved. But why had the box shifted? We continued our search.

Upon lifting the bunk boards of the quarter berth to starboard next to the engine we noticed a cross brace had torn loose at one end and had dropped down, jamming itself against the side of the berth. There was the culprit. The two large storage batteries, each weighing sixty pounds, had sprung the side of the engine box, tearing the brace loose and stopping the engine. With the brace jammed, it would not allow the side of the engine box to spring back and free the flywheel. What a trap. We put everything back together and were relieved that the engine was not harmed and that we had only a small repair job to the bracing in the battery compartment.

The 9th of April arrived but Darryl and Birthe didn't, they had apparently made other plans for the holidays. Ken and I continued building the staging and the cradle. This was very hard, very heavy and very cold work. Progress was slow because of what we had to work with and we were having to venture further and further to find materials. We had used the available boards and timbers close to the boat.

Visitors had gotten word of the disaster and were coming to see us. Most only shook their heads and wondered why we didn't give that boat up and go buy another one. All Americans were rich, were they not?

These were not! Some of the friendly Danes would help by bringing a board or piece of timber as they came up the beach. This was great and much appreciated because our feet were getting terribly bruised from continuously walking on the round, slick stones with heavy loads. We could have used a good pair of hiking boots. They would have to be waterproof though because we were constantly wading in the icy water while working around the boat.

One of our visitors was a medical doctor and asked if we had any injuries. I showed him my hand with the smashed fingers. He did a quick examination and confirmed that the middle finger was broken and needed a splint. I told him that I would not be able to work with a bound up hand and that I was managing. He said I was taking a chance with at least having a crooked finger. I thanked him for his opinion and went back to work.

That evening we knocked off work and stowed our tools. I dug out some clean clothes and got my kit together. It was my time for a hot bath and a meal with our farmer friends and I wanted to be ready, I was really looking forward to it. A few minutes later Sevend and Lars walked up.

Sevend Jorgensen was a master farmer. They lived in a large, spacious house surrounded by a barn, out buildings and farm implements. It was neat and homey looking. Mrs. Jorgensen was preparing a big meal with lots of strange dishes. While she carried on with that, I was shown the bathroom. It had the usual plumbing. The bathtub was a huge, white enamel, cast iron affair.

While the tub filled I took my clothes off and examined my body in the mirror. I was shocked! My sides, from under my arms to my knees were blue and purple. A large swollen welt lay along my left rib cage and looked awful. No wonder I hurt. I was amazed that I was able to move at all.

I ran the tub full of hot steaming water. Then I eased in. Oh what pain, what bliss! Once I got used to the heat it was wonderful. I scrubbed down, drained the water, and did it again. Finally Sevend knocked on the door to make sure that I hadn't drowned. It felt so good I had to force myself to leave. Reluctantly, I put on fresh clothes, and felt like a new person, ready for anything.

The meal that followed was scrumptious, and I ate slowly, savoring every mouthful. That's how the Danes eat, and I must say, it has merit. This was punctuated with small glasses of aquavit; a strong, fiery liquid made from Vodka and caraway seeds. It is the national drink of Denmark, and they love it. It gives the world a rather rosy glow after a while and you tend to relax and enjoy yourself. It all ended too soon. They drove me back to the stairway at the Baron's estate where I bid them goodnight and made my way back to the ship.

When I arrived, I found Darryl, Birthe and Ken finishing off the last of a chicken dinner that the Baron had been so kind to send down by his daughter. It looked as though they had been having a grand time. Our shipwreck had taken on the air of a beach party. It was good to be laughing and smiling again. There was a good feeling of close friendship with all the people who were helping us so much. We would get the ship off the beach.

On the 10th of April, Darryl went to the fishing harbour of Klintholm Havn, only five miles South of our position to try to hire a fishing trawler to pull us off the beach, but no luck.

They couldn't help us. It was too dangerous. The rocks, tides and pilings were just too numerous to even think about. And not only was it dangerous, but the minute they engaged in any kind of a salvage operation their insurance would be cancelled! I couldn't blame them for not risking their livelihood to help a crazy American sailor off the beach.

Well there it was again, and my hunch was proving right; if we wanted the ship off that beach we'd have to do it ourselves.

The anchors were still buried off shore so I decided to use them for pulling power. We had managed to right the ship with them and I figured we could pull *Blue Gipsy* off the beach with them too. It wouldn't be easy, but it could be done...it had to be done.

That night the barometer, which had been steady, suddenly began to fall. I feared for the worst and just when we were ready to launch the boat. I needed only one more day and we'd be off the beach. I was really worried and didn't sleep too good that night. I was up several times to check the barometer and to look at the weather.

By morning I was convinced that the weather, although cold, was stable. Our storm had failed to materialize. Obviously there was something wrong with the barometer. I tapped it for the ten-thousandth time and the hand suddenly became a pendulum, pointing straight down. I guess it got tired of us banging on it every ten minutes. Good! At least I didn't have to worry about its every pulsation. It did remind us though that we should make all haste to get *Blue Gipsy* afloat and away from Moen.

The next day, the 11th, we worked harder than usual to get the ship ready to go. By late that afternoon all was in readiness except for laying her over on the cradle. We decided to wait until the next morning to do that. We both needed a good night's sleep for the ordeal of launching. We knew from experience that sleeping in a heeling boat is not good. It wouldn't take long to lay her over and then we'd have the whole day to get her back into the water.

Suddenly we heard loud talking and laughing and looked up to see a group of about a dozen tough looking men and women walking toward us. They were a friendly and good-natured group. Darryl started talking to them and learned that they were a motorcycle gang on an outing and camped close by. They had walked down to see if there was any way they could help us. We told them yes, that we would try to launch the following day, and could use the extra help. They agreed to come back down and lend a hand.

Darryl and Birthe decided to stay aboard that night. It would save time and give us a good start in the morning. It was a good idea and we had plenty of room. Birthe had found the wayward forehatch cover a mile or so up the beach, and with that in place, the fo'c'sle was dry and comfortable. We enjoyed a meal cooked by Birthe and turned in early. No party that night.

We all got a good night's sleep and were up before dawn for the launch. Birthe cooked a hearty breakfast and cleaned up the galley. We set about unloading much of the heavy gear out of the ship. We also pumped the fresh water tanks dry to make her as light as possible, every pound would count with only muscle power doing the work.

By nine o'clock, all was in readiness. By running a line from the mast to a tree up the cliff we eased *Blue Gipsy* over to seaward on the cradle. Cushions from the forward berths protected the sides of the hull from further damage. Now the real work of launching began.

I took the steel snatch block Darryl had brought and tied it to the end of the anchor line. The anchors were still dug in and should stand the strain of pulling *Blue Gipsy* off the beach. Next, I took a long spare piece of nylon line, 5/8 inch in diameter, and tied it to the point of the cradle. I ran the other end through the snatch block on the anchors and back to the jib track on the deck of *Blue Gipsy*. I passed it through a block there and led it back to the port sheet winch, made three turns around the drum then ran it across the cockpit and around the other winch. This would help distribute the load that we'd be putting on the winches.

Darryl was elected to be winch operator, while Ken and I would handle the rollers and supervise the work gang. At this time there was only three of us.

We were surprised at how heavy *Blue Gipsy* was. I guess this was because we had never been faced with rolling a ten-thousand-pound boat on wooden rollers, but she moved! Darryl winched until the cockpit coaming bowed in and he was afraid that something was going to get torn away. I took a look and put the drop-boards in the companionway to help brace the sides of the cabin and told him to winch away, If the winches pulled out we would just have to rig something else.

Darryl really started cranking; Ken and I used long poles to pry at the keel. The ship moved an inch at a time toward the water. Suddenly from out of nowhere three or four people materialized and were helping to push and pry at the ship; it made a difference! *Blue Gipsy* lumbered toward the edge of the water…and stopped. No amount of shoving, pushing, pulling, or winching would budge her.

We were standing around trying to catch our breath and figure out what to do next when we heard laughing and shouting from up the beach. The motorcycle gang ambled up, took one look and got busy. First they went and scavenged some short, stout pry poles. They used these to pry under the keel and *Blue Gipsy* started to edge seaward once again. One giant of a Viking named Neils kept breaking poles off until finally one chap did nothing

How Do You Salvage a Dream? Very Carefully... 77

but bring more poles, which Neils promptly reduced to firewood.

Finally the ship was far enough out that the work gang started getting their feet wet in the frigid water. Not to be thwarted they started throwing rocks in behind *Blue Gipsy* and built a small levy to work from. It was amazing to see the speed that things got done, not to mention the ingenuity that was shown. All the while they were laughing and joking back and forth. They seemed to be enjoying themselves. But once again *Blue Gipsy* stopped cold...she wouldn't move at all.

I waded out to the end of the cradle and discovered that she had hit a large rock that was too large to move and too high for the cradle to slip over. We'd have to find another way. The water was about three feet deep. My mind raced for a solution. If we got the boat off the cradle, pulled her around until she pointed to sea, we may be able to pull the masthead down and make her float enough to ease past the rocks. It was worth a try. I took the axe and went around to the seaward side of the ship and started chopping at the shoring. With one final whack she suddenly and violently crashed into the sea, throwing up a sheet of spray that covered me with ice water. With the loud sound of splintering, crashing noises ringing in my ears I made my way to the inside of the boat. I was sick at the thought that some bit of shoring or a brace had penetrated the hull. A quick look around under the dinette table showed no water coming in and nothing sticking up inside. I was very thankful for that.

Next I took the line that we were winching with and transferred it from the end of the cradle to the bow of the ship. I also moved the turning block to the bow so that all the pulling force was on the bow. I wanted to rotate *Blue Gipsy* ninety degrees and point her out to sea. Then

I took a long line and tied it to the stern and while Darryl operated the winches, I had the shore gang heave on the stern line. It worked! She was soon pointing to sea.

I needed to get all the shoring and the cradle from under the keel so I took the stern line, waded out and tied it to a piece of the cradle. The shore gang saw, understood, and pulled it out. In a very short while the cradle and bracing were all removed. *Blue Gipsy* lay on her side rocking gently in the small waves. She was practically afloat, heeling about 50 degrees to port.

All was in readiness for the final go. I took the stern line and attached it to the main halyard. Then I motioned for everyone to take hold and pull for all they were worth, this brought the tip of the mast almost down to the water, Darryl and I were both winching in the cockpit and she moved! She bumped and scraped along the bottom, and with every turn of the winches she moved further. With a final bump she was free! The people ashore were unable to hold her down…she was off the beach! There was cheering and hurrahing from shore as the joy of our success spread through the hearts of everyone. I was shivering and blue from wading in the frigid water, but excited and happy to be off that beach. We'd done it!

We made fast to the anchors. I was soaking wet and about to freeze to death so went below for a change of clothes. Next, using the dinghy we ferried all our gear out to the ship. I asked Darryl to invite everyone to the guesthouse at Klintholm Havn for a free dinner and beer party.

Finally all the gear was aboard. Darryl was elected to be our pilot and go with us to Klintholm Havn. We heaved our trusty anchors aboard and motored slowly out through the maze of rocks and piling to deep water. How sweet it was to be away from that dreadful place. We set a course

How Do You Salvage a Dream? Very Carefully... 79

for Klintholm Havn, five miles away to the South.
It was just about dark when we chugged into port.
There was quite a crowd along the quay and eager hands took our lines and greeted us with warm smiles. Then we all walked up to the guesthouse. The Baron was waiting there with several people who had helped us. The Jorgenson family was there too. The word had spread that we were off the beach.

The party went on for hours. We ate fried eels, fish, french fried potatoes, bread, anything and everything, and beer, lots of beer. The guesthouse ran out of food and many of the people left and went home.

Later they ran out of beer and that did it, it was time to pay up and leave. The bill was impressive but worth every Krona. They shooed everyone out and closed the doors, and the party moved down to *Blue Gipsy*.

By then the motorcycle gang was speaking English and I could almost speak Danish. Finally, thankfully, the beer ran out again and everyone drifted away, the party was over.

It was great to be afloat again with the ship safely in port. We had been on the beach one-week exactly. We had learned a lot in that week. We each had lost 20 pounds. Our bodies were on the mend, and so was the ship. Ahead would be other problems, but hopefully nothing to compare with our beaching. Now it was back to Copenhagen for repairs.

CHAPTER SIX
Return to Kastrup

It was clear and cold when I finally roused out of bed. I fired up the cooker and started breakfast while Ken began unloading all the lockers and hauling everything out on the quay. We decided that this was going to be a "drying-out-day"and I wanted to get an early start. At these latitudes, sunny days are in short supply.

By the time we finished eating and washing up, the sun was warm and streaming down. We unloaded everything and laid it out along the quay. The volume was overwhelming to the point of embarrassment. I vowed to send half of it back to the states upon our arrival in Copenhagen.

All the daylong a steady stream of spectators trudged along the quay. Word had spread across the countryside that we were off the beach. We had been in the news and a lot of people were aware of who we were and what had happened. They would come by just to stare at the battered and scarred hull of *Blue Gipsy* and shake their heads in wonderment. Then they would stare at the amount of gear we'd spread out along the quay and shake their heads in amazement. They were a quiet and friendly lot though and wished us well.

We sorted through our collection and tried to fill a trash drum with rejects. The locals found this quite interesting and hauled it away as quick as we dumped it in.

While all our gear was drying in the sun we rerigged the mast; it had taken quite a beating. One of the cleats was torn off and missing. The upper and lower shrouds were slack. The lower mast track recess was squeezed shut from the strain of the anchor line, and the bolt I'd put through the base of the mast, in lieu of the original pin attaching it to the stainless shoe on the cabin top, was bent double like a staple. That little nut and bolt was the only thing that kept the mast on deck throughout the entirety of our ordeal. Without it, the mast would not have lasted five seconds. It would also take some doing to remove it, and we could take care of that when we pulled the mast out in Copenhagen.

Considering what the spars had been through they were still in very good shape. They had survived the worst test anyone could imagine and I was quite proud of my little ship. She had proved herself to be a tough one.

By evening we had tightened the rigging and re-loaded the ship. It was very nice to have everything dry and clean smelling. We began to feel almost normal again. We were still stiff and very sore from the beating we'd taken, gaunt in the face from the weight we had lost, but morale was high and we were in good spirits. We turned in early so we could get a fresh start to Copenhagen in the morning.

JOURNAL ENTRY, April 14, 1971...

A foggy morning out, the promise of a fine sunshiny day. I got breakfast going and Ken filled our water tanks. They had been emptied to lighten the ship. After breakfast and wash-up we cast off and set a course for Copenhagen, fifty miles to the North. The wind was right on the nose at 5 knots, so we motored. The sun burned the fog and the little diesel chugged along without missing a beat. It took ten hours to make the trip, but we enjoyed the lazy, lolling around in the warm sun. It felt good to our battered bodies and spirits. Finally, and once again, we tied to the quay in the little yacht harbour of Kastrup. Was it only ten days ago that we had sailed? It seemed a lot longer than that.

The next day I caught a cab to Baess' office and talked with him about getting the ship repaired. He said that everyone felt badly about our misadventure and would do all they could to get us ship-shape and on our way. I was a bit testy over his lack of response to my plea for help. I made my point and dropped it. Such is life.

We moved on and he assured me that they would haul *Blue Gipsy* first thing the next morning and begin repairs immediately. I thanked him and took a cab back to the harbour.

After lunch Pally and his wife Connie (two members of the motorcycle gang) dropped by and we rode over to Darryl and Birthe's apartment. The giant, Neils, and his wife Lona showed up, then more members and their friends until there was quite a party going on. I've never known people so ready to party. I broke away at 11PM and headed back to the ship. The cold wind and the two-mile walk cleared my head. I turned in and slept so soundly I didn't wake up when Ken came back aboard.

The next morning we used the boom on the quay to pull the mast, then motored over to the railway. True to Baess' word *Blue Gipsy* was hauled, and immediately placed in a shed at the end of the ways. Ken and I unloaded our gear and piled it in one corner of the shed.

Then we lent a hand opening up the interior of the ship. The workmen had to get at the nuts and bolts holding the bow pulpit and the starboard toe rail on. These would be replaced. That evening we checked into a nearby hotel.

The next few days were rather hectic; parties at night, groggy mornings, and problems of every kind. Baess was talking about launching by Friday, but they were only fixing the outside of the ship—no repairs to the inside. I finally got fed up with the double talk and demanded an explanation. He confessed that they were not going to fix the inside of the hull—It was beyond their expertise; they were only going to fix the gel-coat on the outside, replace the toerail, the pulpit, do some minor cosmetics and that was it!

This was news to me. I had talked to him about getting several estimates on the repairs from other yards including the firm that molded the hull. But Baess assured me that they would be able to handle anything that came up. I was not trying to get a free ride. I was willing to pay for all repairs.

I really got upset and in somewhat of a dangerous mood—I had run out of patience. "What do you want me to do?" he asked. I told him that I would fix the boat. Time was running out and whatever was going to be done would have to be done quickly. To calm me down he offered me the use of the whole shop, and we could do whatever we wanted to do. They would come down in the morning, open up and leave. We could help ourselves to anything and everything. This suited me just fine.

The next morning we were waiting at the door when a chap came with the keys. He unlocked the shop and all the cabinets then left. I started right away cutting and fitting several layers of fiberglass matt and cloth to the inside of the hull, especially around the fractures. There were several other areas that needed beefing up too. The longitudinal stiffener to which everything is attached was also fractured in several places on the starboard side. It was tough, working up behind the cabinets, but I took my time. I had to do a good job—we were the ones going to sea in her.

Later I had Sanderson, the chap who builds the hull, come down and look at the work. He said that it was exactly what they would have done, but they would have painted the whole boat. I was not interested in a paint job. I only wanted to have a sound repair and to be gone).

That night someone broke into the shed and stole quite a few items of clothing and cassette tapes. We called the police and caused quite a stir at the boat yard. Apparently it was an inside job and "Ivan the Russian" had gone missing. He was one of the workmen at the yard. Apparently he removed a board from the wall of the shop, took what he wanted, slipped away and skipped town. Fortunately he didn't take anything essential to the voyage. We sorted through all the gear one more time and shipped two heavy footlockers back to the states. Most of it was bulky winter clothes and books. It gave us some much-needed room and lightened the ship considerably.

At a party I met a doctor and told him the trouble I was having with my hands. The skin was peeling off and they were very tender, also I had no feeling in the ends of my fingers. I'd have to take everything out of my pocket to find a coin. It was very annoying. He said that we had suffered nerve damage from the prolonged exposure to the cold, and that it would take several months for the nerves to heal. That eased my mind considerably. They would heal. I felt much better about it.

My broken finger was mending too. I had gotten in the habit of not using it and that helped. It did make working difficult at times, but I was just glad to be alive. The bruises disappeared and we gradually returned to normal, none-the-worse for wear.

Friday, April 23...

Blue Gipsy slid back down the ways. It lacked the excitement and fanfare of the first launch, but I was happy. The weather was gray and stormy. We lost no time in checking out of the hotel and moving back aboard. Then we immediately set to work on the ship. The weather forecast called for heavy winds and I wanted to get the mast back in before they arrived, otherwise it would be impossible. We just made it. By the time we completed the job it was blowing 25 knots, very cold and we were glad to be tied to the quay.

During the next few days we rushed about getting mail, paying bills and buying the last few items of gear. We invested in some waterproof, slipover gloves and a better set of rain gear with a pullover top. During our ordeal the wind would unsnap the front of the famous, brand name rain parkas we were wearing. (That was one reason we became so wet and cold). We also bought heavy raw-wool fisherman's sweaters. We had learned a few things and were not going to be cold all the time anymore.

CHAPTER SEVEN
If at First You Don't Succeed...

The 28th of April rolled up and I had had it. Ken was partying and drinking excessively every night. He would stumble in well after midnight and go to bed, then sleep it off later and later. It was not a good day to leave, but it was that time. The weather was going to be squally, with some rain and snow. Visibility was marginal—maybe a mile. Ken was asleep, so I simply cranked the engine, untied the lines and we were off…Klintholm Havn would be our first stop.

    Ken was not able to do anything and stayed in his bunk until noon. I scurried around with sails, heating water for tea, coffee, or hot chocolate, preparing lunch and navigating. I was pleased to see that the self-steering gear was working much better. Before, it steered erratically due to excessive weather helm. We had corrected a lot of this by moving the mast slightly forward when we re-installed it. Now the ship was quite easy to steer. Ken finally got up and kept a tiller watch just to make sure we stayed on course. He seemed to be feeling better.

    We were about five miles from the entrance to the harbour at Klintholm Havn when I noticed fishing boats passing us in a flurry. It was cloudy and the wind had picked up. Off to starboard I could see our dreadful beach just below the towering dirty-white cliffs of Moen. A shiver went up my spine and I had to mentally shake off the rush of unpleasant thoughts that came into my mind. All this was forgotten when I glanced to windward and saw tops of waves being blown off by strong gusts of wind! Oh no, here we are in the same place two weeks later with the same situation developing. I dashed below and got into my warmest clothes, then pulled on my foul weather gear. Next I cranked the engine and set it to half throttle. Back in the cockpit I told Ken to go down and get prepared too. We were in for another wild ride.

The self-steering was holding a good course but the ship was hard pressed. I went forward and lowered the main sail, furled it and secured it to the boom. Now we had only the working jib pulling and that could be doused quickly should the need arise. I had learned a few things and had no intention of making the same mistakes again. You learn lessons from failures.

The waves grew quickly and the wind came on stronger. Heavy dark clouds scudded low on the horizon. The whole scene took on a sinister and wild look. This is what sent the fishermen running for the safety of Klintholm Havn! By the time we arrived at the harbour entrance visibility was down to a quarter mile, with snow flurries.

Waves were setting up a surge in the entrance to the harbour but it was nothing compared to what we'd been through only two weeks ago. I went forward, lowered and bagged the jib. Then I dogged the hatches. Out in the cockpit I released the self-steering and took over the tiller and steered for the safety of that snug harbour.

We shot through the breakwater to the calm waters inside. There was an empty slip on the South side of the quay. We rigged every fender we had to the starboard side and tied *Blue Gipsy* securely to the big iron rings set in the concrete of the quay. We'd made it.

We lost no time in securing everything topside and went below to the warm, cozy cabin of our little ship. I prepared a hearty meal and we thankfully sat down to eat and savored every bite. How sweet it was to be snug and secure in port while outside the storm raged.

We stayed in port the following day. The sleet and snow piled up on the cockpit lockers until it spilled over the coaming. The wind moaned in the rigging and at times it was strong enough to heel *Blue Gipsy* over 10 to 15 degrees. We kept busy with lots of small jobs inside the ship and only ventured out once. The mooring lines were chafing on the edge of the concrete quay and we had to place chafing gear (bits of cloth) under them. It was very cold out there and we worked fast.

Repairing the dinette table was a priority item. We'd smashed it flat during our trip to the beach and I had just sort of stuck it back together. I dug out glue and screws and made a proper repair. Next, I installed a down-latch on the support leg of the table and that made it very stable. It was right across from the stove and you leaned on it while on the starboard tack and on port tack you more or less clung to it. I also rigged an adjustable burner on the little gimbaled stand-by stove that hung on the bulkhead. That was the stove that clogged up and went out while we were getting beat half to death on the anchor line at Moen. The adjustable burner had a built-in pricking mechanism that quickly took care of any stoppage in the jet.

That night the storm began to abate and we looked forward to getting away the next day.

Rodby Havn was our next port, sixty miles away on the island of Lolland. We left Klintholm Havn at daylight and had a mixed bag of sailing and motoring. The winds switched around so fast we could only sail a short while before we'd have to tack or run the engine to keep up with our way points. We did not want to be out after dark because the fog usually rolled in. But we made it in due time and were safely tied next to the quay by 5:30 PM.

It was early, and with plenty of daylight left Ken decided to hike the mile to a grocer. He bought beer, bread and eggs. We ate supper and turned in. It had been a long day and tomorrow we'd push on to Kiel, Germany and the canal.

May 1, 1971...

The wind was very light so we motored out of the harbour at Rodby Havn and set our course for Kiel. The wind continued to be flunky all day and it was an exercise in motor sailing. Of course the shipping was very heavy and at one time I counted twenty-one large ships.

The last mile or so we had a strong breeze and had a fine sail all the way to the British Kiel Yacht Club dock. We lowered, furled and bagged our sails, and tied up next to a beat-up wooden thirty foot sloop flying an East German flag from her stern. We had arrived in Kiel.

It seemed as though our intrusion of German waters had gone completely unnoticed. Our "Q" flag was flying and we just sat on the ship awaiting developments. A blond head appeared in the companionway of the sloop and one Gerhard Schlenker came over for a gam.

Gerhard was a student of engineering at the university nearby and lived aboard the old sloop to beat the high cost of housing. After graduation he had hopes of rebuilding her and doing some more extensive sailing. We were still flying our yellow "Q" flag and I asked Gerhard where the customs and immigrations were located. He pointed out some government docks across the bay.

Gerhard spoke excellent English and offered to pilot us over and be our interpreter. The breeze was still with us so we motored away from the dock and set the main and working jib. It was quite nice to have someone else do the navigating while we enjoyed a leisurely sail around the harbour. Gerhard was a good sailor and thoroughly enjoyed being at the helm of *Blue Gipsy*. He noticed the electronic log was registering too high and mentioned it to me. I agreed. It was also distracting because there was also a two-knot speed difference between port and starboard tacks. Excess baggage it was, and on *Blue Gipsy*, "If you don't work you don't ride." I vowed to get rid of it at first opportunity.

We docked at a long concrete pier. The small corrugated iron building on top looked out of place. On the roof, "ZOLL" was painted in big green letters. Gerhard went up and explained our position to the uniformed official at the desk. He gave me some papers to sign and asked if we had any cigarettes or bonded stores. We didn't. In German he said, "Fine, no problem." He really didn't seem too interested. We cast off and had a pleasant sail back to the Yacht Club and tied up alongside Gerhard's sloop.

By now we were all hungry. Our new friend suggested a nearby guesthouse that had good food at a reasonable price. It felt good to walk about after being confined to the ship for so long. Gerhard ordered eggs, while Ken and I had a snitzel with potatoes and vegetables. Thick-crusted bread and fine German beer rounded off the meal. (We were eating a lot more than normal, but I think our bodies were trying to gain back the weight we'd lost. Not to mention the healing process which takes a lot of sustenance). The food was fine in quality and quantity and we thoroughly enjoyed it. Afterwards, I paid the bill and we walked back to the ship.

I broke out the sherry and we spent the evening talking and telling stories of our adventures. By 2200 we were so tired we could hardly keep our eyes open. Gerhard took his leave and we turned in for some much-needed rest. It had been a very busy day.

The next day was sunny and warm so we decided to take the day off for some much needed R&R. The area around the entrance to the Canal was interesting being made up of several small villages. I thought that it would be grubby and sooty from industry and shipping but not so. The houses are quaint and brightly colored in rows as neat as a card of buttons. The locks themselves are located in the little town of Holtenau.

We asked Gerhard if he'd like to go along and he accepted. He was an excellent guide and we had a very pleasant time. He took us to the locks and showed us how the signal lights worked, the office where we had to pay our tonnage fee and a wealth of other information. We had a grand time of it and decided to round it off with a sail.

We walked back to the ship, cast off the lines and put up the main and jenny. There was a nice breeze and we sailed over next to the locks. I wanted to see them from the water. Tomorrow we would have to lock through and that was serious business. I didn't want any mishaps. We enjoyed a most pleasant two hours, then sailed back and tied up.

While Ken and Gerhard stowed the gear I lit the stove and prepared supper...hash brown potatoes with a fried egg on top, sausage on the side, washed down with beer. Afterwards being tired out we bid Gerhard farewell and turned in.

    I planned on pulling out early the next morning. We would need the whole day to transit the canal. I had never experienced locking through and was naturally a bit apprehensive about the whole process. I wanted to be fresh and alert when we arrived in the morning.

CHAPTER EIGHT
Passage of the Kiel Canal...

The night went all too fast and by 0400 we were up and having breakfast. Excitement filled the clear, early morning air. It was going to be a beautiful, sunny day. I saw Gerhard wave to us as we pulled away. "Goodbye, and good luck!" We waved back and turned our full attention to the locks.

The signal light glowed green in the early dawn of the morning. No other traffic moved so we motored right into the lock. The lockmaster directed us to tie next to a fishing boat and the crew took our lines, So far so good. I asked Ken to take the ships papers and go pay our tonnage fee for passage through the canal. The lock doors began to close slowly behind us. A few minutes later Ken came hurrying back aboard with the news that he didn't have enough money for the 15 DM. fee and they would not take US dollars. By this time the lock doors were closed and they were starting to flood the lock! I took the ships papers and went up to the controller. He said they would give me change in the souvenir shop. I ran, there was a line. I waited my turn and changed five dollars to marks. Then I ran back to the controller (who seemed rather amused by all the fuss) and shoved the money at him. He took it and gave me a receipt. I ran back to the ship and jumped aboard as the doors swung wide open.

Ken looked rather distraught; he didn't like maneuvering and docking *Blue Gipsy* any way. But to be thrust into the prospect of leaving me and heading out of the locks alone, with a ship and four fishing boats was a bit much. The crew on the fishing boat cast our lines off and gave us a shove. The lockmaster motioned for us to go and we moved out like a rabbit with a pack of hounds in hot pursuit.

Vessels in the canal are not supposed to overtake and pass another vessel but we were not up to the pace. We could probably manage the speed but why go through the stress of being in the lead? There was deep water right to the edge of the canal so I pulled over as far as I could and throttled back enough to let the other traffic ease by. Soon the others were out of sight around a bend or two and we were for the most part alone.

The warm rays of a bright sun burned off the misty damp and coldness of morning. It felt so good on our bodies so we took off our coats, then our sweaters, and soon we were down to t-shirts. Oh what bliss…warm at last!

We saw deer in the brush along the canal. Insects were buzzing and there were plenty of birds flitting around. Small villages flanked the canal but the high banks let us see only the highest chimneys and steeples. Ships and fishing boats met us in groups. They came from every port of the world. We saw our first Russian ship and waved at the five crewmen on deck. Only one waved back.

The shipping became steady but was not a problem. Ships over a certain tonnage must have a pilot on board, and there's a five knot speed limit during transit of the canal. (It seemed faster than that to me.) This keeps things

Ashore on Moen

One sad Ship

Blocked up on Moen

Relaunching

Motorcycle gang helped push

Careening and hauling off

Launched!

Hauling gear out to Blue Gipsy

White cliffs of Moen

Ken and I, tired but Relieved

The Baron, center

Drying out a Klintholm Havn

North Sea fishing boat, Klintholm Havn

Repairs at Kastrup

Stepping the mast, #2

Back to Kintholm Havn in sleet and snow

Kiel Canal

Snow Maiden

Falmouth, England

Fresh mackerel

Serious Navigation

Fishing float

Land Ho!

Lateen rigged Grand Canary Boat

moving in an orderly and professional manner.
By late afternoon we were approaching the North Sea end of the canal. The lock was open and we pulled in and tied up next to a big German tug. The lock doors closed and we were let down to the level of the harbour and the doors opened. The chap on the tug let our lines go and we shoved off. I eased ahead and started out of the lock but the lock master shouted through a loud hailer that you could have heard in Kiel, "American yacht hold your position!"

Oh me! I tried my best, but as the other vessels pulled out, we were thrown about by their prop wash. I'll never understand why he did this because it was very dangerous for us and we came very close to hitting the side of a ship and then the side of the lock as we were thrown first this way then that. I think it was simply free entertainment. But presently it was our turn and we were waved out of the lock. We both breathed a deep sigh of relief.

The town of Brunsbuttle hosts the North Sea end of the Kiel Canal and lies several miles up the broad and muddy Elbe River. Gerhard had said that there was a guesthouse and dock just outside the locks, and sure enough we swung right, then up a narrow channel to a float. A beautiful green lawn with cement steps led up to the guesthouse. After securing everything we trudged up the steep steps, went inside and over a half-liter of good German beer ordered a meal. In typical German efficiency it arrived post haste. We ate slowly and enjoyed it. We were tired. It had been a very long and somewhat stressful day.

The proprietor of the guesthouse was also the harbormaster and for the fee of 5 DM per day assigned us a space at the float. He was a most congenial man and spoke excellent English. He told us that a lot of the canal pilots and ships captains came here for a meal or a drink. By the time we'd finished eating, several had come in and were talking. One of them spoke to us and asked where we were headed. "Otterndorf," we replied, because it's where Ken's family were from. (His grandfather had migrated from there in the early 1900's.) It was not far away, they assured us, only five or six kilometers down and across the Elbe from where we were tied up. I needed a chart of the area but they were not sure where I could pick up one locally. They explained, apologetically, that Brunsbuttel was only a small town and did not have a chart agency.

We spent a very pleasant evening talking and drinking "corn" with those friendly men. "Corn" is a clear liqueur having a pleasant fresh taste with a hint of turpentine. Every so often one of the men would tap slowly and deliberately three times on the table with his middle finger, tap-tap-tap. This signaled the end of that round of drinks and the beginning of the next. Everyone drank up. The fiery stuff went down smoothly, followed by a quiet explosion way down in the stomach, then a feeling of great warmth that traveled back up to your head and face, especially the ears. It was a very strange sensation. I'm glad it was down hill to *Blue Gipsy*.

We both slept in the next morning. I thought I would have a terrific hangover but not so. I felt fine and cooked a big breakfast of eggs, sausage, toast, tea and coffee. After the dishes were washed, dried and put away we had a second cup of coffee and discussed the plans for the day. We needed some bread, as always, and a few other things. But more importantly, I needed that chart so we could get up the channel to Otterndorf. Tides in the area ran six feet or so with plenty of shallow water. In fact, we couldn't even leave the float unless it was half-tide or more. But search as we did in the little town of Brunsbuttel we could not come up with a chart. The rest of the day was spent tidying up and drying out the ship. It was strange not having to run the stove all day to keep warm. It was very pleasant in fact.

That evening we went back to the guesthouse for dinner and talked to the harbormaster. I explained to him that I desperately needed a chart but had been unable to locate one. He said that he had an atlas of charts and that it would be very easy to make a tracing of that particular area, and that is exactly what I did. We walked to his office, I borrowed his atlas and all the materials, sat down and traced the area I needed. A neat trick that I have used many times since.

It was Wednesday, May 5, 1971. The wind was from astern, brisk and cold. After clearing the harbour I raised the working jib and main, and trimmed them wing and wing. We were going like a train. "Watch for the trees," the harbormaster had warned, "They mark the channel up to Otterndorf." The local fishermen and sailors cut saplings and stick them down in the muddy bottom to mark the ever-changing channel. I could see how easy it would be to get swept up on the mud flats in the swift current of the mighty Elbe.

A narrow channel cut through the banks of the river and we could see some buildings and docks with various sail and powerboats about a half-mile further on. I took the sails off and started the engine. There was a fork in the canal and we took the right one; to the left was a lock and several narrow, steel canal boats waiting to lock through. It was a man-powered lock and I have no idea where the canal went. We'd gone about a hundred feet and had two hundred yards to go, when I felt the keel touch bottom. The depth sounder went from 8 feet to four and we came to a firm stop. I reversed the engine and opened the throttle wide, We didn't budge. Ken took the whisker pole and tried to shove off. It only sank into the soft mud bottom and came up dribbling black sticky goo on the deck. Then I rigged our smallest anchor and tried several times to heave it out far enough to set, but to no avail. The tide was falling fast and we were not moving. In fact, we were starting to list to one side. Suddenly there was a small motor launch right in front of us. He swung around smartly and threw a line. Ken caught it, belayed it around the bow cleat, and with a burst of power we were dragged off the mud and back into the channel. We followed the launch back to the dock and tied up next to a neat German motorsailer. There was no open dock space available.

While I cleaned up and stowed away, Ken made his way up to the guesthouse and called his relatives. I followed him a bit later and met a Mister Stephens, the chap who pulled us off the mud. I sheepishly thanked him for coming to our rescue. He laughed and said it was part of the harbormaster's job. The channel was tricky and lots of skippers made that same mistake. Ken came up and said that his people would be down a bit later. Otterndorf was a few miles away and they would have to organize transportation.

Back aboard *Blue Gipsy*, The motorsailer pulled out and headed back for Brunsbuttle so we took his spot at the dock. With company coming we straightened up the ship and changed to fresh clothes. We wanted to look our best. Then we walked back up to the guesthouse for a beer.

The lounge was on the second floor and you could see for miles in all directions. I noticed that the motorsailer was aground out near the entrance to the channel. Another small sloop pulled out and ran aground in about the same place we did. The harbormaster had left for home so they would be there through the tide. I felt sorry for them, but felt better that locals got stuck in the mud too.

During the next three days we were treated like royalty, wined and dined by Ken's happy family. They took us to meet people all around the area. One of the most memorable sights was the sandbars off Cruxhaven. There was a guesthouse out there a mile or more off shore and tourists would ride the special horse drawn wagons out for dinner. The wagons had enormous wheels and only the very biggest, best horses were used to haul them. In the time it took to go out to the guesthouse, eat a meal, and come back, the tide would be up to the horses' belly. Quite exciting really. We could also see the rusty hulk of a grounded ship out there on the sand...a grim reminder to me that navigating through that maze of sand and strong tides was going to be tough, even without the fog and poor visibility.

As I stood there at Cruxhaven in the cold wind, looking out across that expanse of windswept sand and swirling water, I couldn't help but contemplate the time that lay just ahead of us, when we'd be out there. Could I do it? Did I have the knowledge and determination to carry it through? We'd find out soon enough. I turned and walked back to the car.

CHAPTER NINE
Trials of the North Sea...

May 8, 1971...Ken's folks came down to see us off and it was mid-morning before we motored away from the dock and out through the tricky channel to the Elbe. I was somewhat apprehensive. This was going to be a tough leg of the voyage. We were fairly well rested but only because Ken's relatives were very settled family folk, and not like the fun loving Danes who party all the time. I knew that we'd need all the strength we could muster to keep out of trouble. The tide was with us and we were making good time.

The wind was light and variable so we just kept the engine running and headed for the lightship off Cruxhaven. Visibility was good and I could see the town in the distance. I could also see that stranded ship, and that, along with the cloudy, overcast skies threw a shroud of sadness and uncertainty over me. I did my best to shake it off Then got busy with the charts and navigation.

I had several excellent German charts of the North Sea, and they showed a string of buoys all the way from Kiel to the English channel and this was punctuated by lightships about every thirty miles. These in turn were in the list of lights and a book of radio navigational aids gave us the call sign and frequency of all the light ships and beacons. Each lightship had a radio transmitter that sent out a strong signal at certain intervals, a signal that we would be able to home in on. This was how we would stay on course should the fog roll in; and the fog *would* roll in.

We fairly flew past Cruxhaven with the strong, muddy current of the Elbe whisking us along. I estimated the speed of the current to be 4.5 knots. As we passed the lightship I saw that they had a storm warning hoisted…two black cones. I swung the helm over and tried to come close alongside, but the current was too strong and I could barely hold my relative position. I shouted at them, "Is there a storm on the way?" And they shouted back…"No, no, we never take the signal down." I thanked them and put the helm over and soon they were hull down on the horizon. I felt even gloomier than before.

There was a steady stream of ships heading up toward Kiel and more than a few coming down behind us. They all tooted their horns at us but I stayed just outside the string of buoys. The water was deep enough for us, but the ships had to keep to the channel. We motored all day and at times there wasn't enough wind to keep the exhaust fumes away from the ship. We'd almost gag from stifling diesel exhaust. We decided that at night we'd keep watch, four hours on and four off. This would keep someone at the helm and give us enough time to sleep and keep up with the chores. During the day one of us would always be topside looking around doing odd jobs and the like, but at night it needed a bit more regimen. I took the 8 to 12, Ken took the 12 to 4, and I came on again for the 4 to 8. This gave Ken more rest. I get along fine with 6 hours sleep. It would give me time to cook breakfast too. Ken would normally get up around 8:00 AM anyway. He'd take the helm and I'd get the stove fired up and a meal on the way.

We both thought the system would work fine.

At about 10:00 PM that night the fog suddenly rolled in. I saw a buoy flashing about half-a-mile in front of us and it just vanished. I kept my course and when the buoy re-appeared I had to steer around to avoid hitting it. I was happy that the compass was good enough to steer by, but dismayed that visibility was almost zero. The fog was so heavy that the masthead light cast only a weak circle of light, which clung to us as we chugged through the thick, swirling mass of fog. It was nerve wracking. At times ships blew their bellowing fog signals right next to us, and at times not. We would only see a faint string of lights streaming close by and hear the swish of the bow cutting through the icy black waters of the North Sea. And the grand finale was that blasted stern wave that would tower up out of the night like some great sea serpent and invade our little bubble of light. If the ship was overtaking we would present the stern, but if head-on the bow and it would smash down sending sheets of cold spray into the air. We quickly learned to take cover behind the dodger and avoid getting the worst of it. Down below it was quite traumatic. If you should be sleeping you would certainly wake up and wonder if we weren't perhaps going over Niagara Falls. If awake, the one on watch would call a warning, "Hang on!" and indeed you had better hang on.

If the ship was overtaking us the wave would come up astern and make *Blue Gipsy* twist and gyrate, throwing the wind out of the sails and the ship off course. It would take a while to get things settled down again. We came to actually hate those waves. It was very disturbing.

The night wore on and finally it was light enough to see the gray misty walls of our bubble. But it was well after sun up before the fog burned off and then suddenly it was very clear, with miles of visibility. We were still on course

and there were still plenty of full-grown ships coming and going at regular intervals. It never let up.
   During the day I discovered that the tides almost matched our hull speed. I was hoping that they would slack off somehow but they didn't. We plugged along just outside the shipping channel and actually sailed some and napped to stay rested up for the ordeal ahead. Sure enough, the next night was a repeat of the first. Just after dark the fog rolled in and navigation became very trying. However, I'd gotten very proficient with the directional finding radio, and we both kept a keen eye on the compass. Winds for the most part were light and variable so we motored a lot and motorsailed otherwise. We did not complain.
   The tides were something else. They didn't seem to make any sense at all. For instance, it took us twenty-one hours under power to run the thirty-miles between the lightships *Tel Schellinger* and *Texel*. I thought maybe we were aground or something. But we finally crept up on it.
   On the morning of May 11th we were in dense fog, low on fuel, had no wind, and were very tired. Neither of us was getting much sleep and especially me because I did all the navigating. The fog really worked on Ken's nerves. He looked bad from the stress of it all. I got the charts out and searched for a hole to duck into. We needed a breather.
   A far as I could tell we were about thirty miles from the port of Ymuiden, Holland. I decided to put in there. I didn't have a chart of the harbour but we'd just take it easy and see how it went. We altered course 90 degrees and followed the radio signal right to the locks.
   Once again I did not want to lock through, but there was no other way to get a rest and fuel. We tied up to a government dock long enough to inquire about what to

do. They told us to motor into the lock when the light turned green. I did, and tied up next to a small freighter. The locks closed and the lockmaster shouted for me to move across to the other side and tie up next to a fishing boat. Oh me, here we go again. The lock was not big enough to maneuver around in. I wished that he could have given a demonstration on how to get a sailboat to go sideways. I pulled up and back, using every trick I knew to get her over to that fishing boat, and I did too. It was not very funny to me, although everyone else found it quite entertaining. Finally we were secure with five or six other vessels and the locks were flooded and we motored out into the canals of Holland.

The yacht marina, we were told, was just inside the canal to port, and sure enough it was. It was so close to the locks that you could toss a stone and hit a ship, but the tug captains were quiet and very efficient when helping ships to negotiate the locks. For our entire stay there not once did I see them have any difficulty. The drill was like this…a huge ship would approach the lock with a big hefty tug of sixty feet on either side with a single cable to the stern of the ship, like two whale calves next to their mother. Then the ship would slowly be swallowed up in the lock until the tugs were about to be scraped off at the gate. Then a whistle would sound and each tug in unison would turn out and away from the ship. Mind you the single towing cable from the stern of each tug is still tied to the stern of the ship. Quite rapidly they would be heeling over and being taken in tow stern first by the ship, but just before the tugs touched they would pour on the power acting as brakes to keep the ship from going right out the other end of the lock. I never tired of watching them perform this nautical ballet.

The marina had a mixed bag of private power and

sailboats. We had no problem getting a slip. It was late and we were both exhausted so I cooked up a quick meal and after we ate, we washed up and turned in.

Ymuiden, I was told, is about two hours from Amsterdam by water. It's a dirty port with a steel mill close by that belched tons of soot into the air and from the looks of things, most of it fell on the boats in the marina. The town itself was about two miles away and much cleaner. (We enjoyed the walks to the grocer and viewed it as an opportunity to stretch our legs and get a bit of exercise. Something we came to miss being onboard all the time).

Quaint little steep-roofed houses standing shoulder to shoulder along narrow twisting streets was Ymuiden. A delightful village with even more delightful people, very quietly spoken, very polite, and surprisingly enough, most of them spoke English. We changed some money, then went shopping for a few groceries; we were always low on bread and took lots of time in the bread shops trying to decide what we'd like. The choices were amazing and it was all very good.

I wanted to get away on the 13th, but the bonded stores I had ordered were late coming down. When they did arrive there was a customs officer with them and he announced that he would have to seal the stowage locker. The only place we could find that suited him was the port cockpit seat. I had to take the hand drill and bore a hole in the bronze latch so he could insert the wire of the seal and then crimp it. But it all went smoothly and then he took off his hat and became a friendly Dutchman. We broke out some beer, bread and cheese and while we munched and drank he told us all about the town and its people. He'd lived there all his life and had been in the customs service 25 years. He left an hour later and wished us good sailing.

After he left we washed up the dishes and hosed the grit and grim off the ship. Then we invited a beautiful young lady from the boat next door over for a drink. Herma was a charming college girl, home for a break and staying aboard the boat in front of us with her mother and father. We had a very nice visit until her father came for her about dark. Ken and I had a snack with a cup of chocolate and turned in. We were tired and wanted to rest up for what we knew lay ahead, and that being the very swift and treacherous English Channel. We had no illusions, and it would be an ordeal. The English Channel is the busiest shipping lane in the world, and one of the roughest and most dangerous.

CHAPTER TEN
Dover Straits and England...

On the morning of May 14 we pulled away from the Ymuiden marina. Everything went smoothly and we locked through out into the frigid waters of the North Sea. We motored for an hour or so before a breeze came up from astern. I set the main and jenny, running them out wing and wing. We began to sail. It's always a treat to shut the engine down, its so quiet and no exhaust fumes to breath, just the soothing sounds of the ship under sail.

The dense fog had raised havoc with shipping in the area and the BBC reported several minor collisions and a tanker aground at Goodwin Sands, near the mouth of the English Channel. That was not good news and only heightened our apprehension of what lay ahead.

I had spent some time assembling an electric foghorn in Kastrup and had no clue as to where I'd gotten the idea. But its time had come and a few more minutes' work would make it operational. Up until now we'd not had a pressing need for it. No coastal traffic to speak of, and the big ships had been totally committed to the deep-water channel. We in turn, stayed completely out of the channel. When I thought we needed to give a fog signal I blew the lung-powered tooter. The English Channel was a whole new ball game. There was lots of open water and hundreds of smaller, coastal craft criss-crossing the steamer routes at every angle day and night, and they travel in any kind of weather. Not to mention blinding fast hovercraft and hydrofoil ferries running between France and England. I wanted to be able to blow the proper signal and to be heard.

Using a small 12-volt automotive horn air compressor, I clamped it to the lower portion of an old electric hand drill whose motor had burned out. I used the lower portion of the housing consisting of the pistol grip and switch and cord…the motor fit snugly in the half round housing. On top of that, using hose clamps, I mounted two stubby air horns. The wires were hooked up, a plug installed on the end and we were ready for a test flight. It was an awesome looking thing, and quite compact, all things considered. I plugged it into the 12-volt receptacle, aimed and pulled the trigger! The amount of sound that came forth was incredible. It's a good thing you could hold it at arms length and point it away from the ship. There was no doubt that we would be heard. I was delighted with it. We called it, "the fog blaster."

That night, true to form the fog rolled in. I got busy with navigation and the foghorn. Sleep was impossible. We were on a treadmill suspended in fog. Steer by the glow of the compass, point the fog-blaster and let go with the proper toots, listen for a response. Eyes straining, ears tuned to catch any sound that would warn of us of approaching danger. I also had to stay on the radio constantly checking and plotting our progress to the next light ship or way-point.

I kept the kettle on and we consumed gallons of hot tea and coffee and chocolate, trying to stay awake and alert and trying to stay warm as well. The fog wet everything and slowly crept through our foul weather gear, wetting our clothes. It was awful.

There were many ships of all sizes going every which way and if that wasn't problem enough all the junk in the water was. We were working our way through the Straits of Dover and as it got light enough to see, we could see tons of flotsam and jetsam of every description in the water. We had to constantly steer around debris; logs, shipping crates, pallets, oil drums, you name it and it was floating around. Fortunately it was daylight enough that we could see and steer through this particular area. Somehow we missed it all. It would have been a different story if we had been there at night, or in rough weather, or both. I didn't want to think about it and I was very thankful that we could see.

A little later Ken was at the helm and I was below trying to get a radio bearing on the next light ship, *Royal Sovereign*. Suddenly the radio went haywire. Nothing made sense. It was all but impossible to get a good "null," and when I did the line was way off from our last position. I broke out in a cold sweat. We really needed and relied on that radio; what could be the matter?

We had no choice but to carry on from our last known position. The compass was all we could rely on. We prayed that the radio itself was all right and that things would clear up soon. Perhaps it was only ground effect or some other atmospheric disturbance that was causing the problem. Finally our prayers were answered as the radio signals became stronger and I managed to sort things out; I was happy to discover that we were still on course and right where we should be. We had not gotten lost. We breathed a deep sigh of relief. Those two hours were the most hectic and confounding since Moen.

The fog-blaster worked great! We'd sound our series of blasts and from somewhere out there a ship would answer our signal. They would slow down and we'd hardly dare to breathe until we were clear of each other...then the beat of their engines would increase and they would continue on their way. The fog was demoralizing. I felt like a rabbit in a bush with the hounds sniffing around. It made you want to run for a safe hole. There were no safe burrows out there, only our little ship pushing our bubble along as we chugged on, our eyes and ears straining to see or hear the next ship.

Then it started to rain. I rigged lines to the tiller so that we could sit in the companionway. We placed a cushion on top of one drop-board and peered through the window of the dodger. We kept the little Primus cooker going below which helped to dry us out and keep us warm. Life would have been bleak indeed without the dodger and the cooker.

The morning of May 16 put us off the Isle of Wight. The fog had burned off and visibility was several miles, under cloudy and overcast gray skies. It was still raining occasionally.

We managed to do some sailing when the wind picked up. We stayed in close to shore and stayed well clear of the shipping lanes. It was such a relief to not have the fog. We were actually beginning to enjoy our trip. We both felt a sense of having rounded the mark and putting the worst behind us. We began to look forward to better sailing and not so much fog.

Our reverie was short-lived. At sundown the wind switched around until it was blowing right on the nose. Thankfully the fog stayed away. That night we sat off Portland Bill for hours with the engine running at full throttle to keep the strong current from sweeping us back up the channel. I estimated the current at four-and-a-half to five knots. The wind stayed right on our nose. I left the main up and sheeted flat to keep the ship from rolling so much. The English Channel is always rough, churned up no doubt from the heavy shipping if nothing else.

At this point I was careful to keep well off shore. There is a bad tiderip that makes out from Portland Bill and we had been warned that small boats could get trapped in it. If the wind falls light and they have no engine they can't break out of it. The sharp, steep wave action knocks all the wind out of the sails and they thrash about until they either sink or the tide changes. We were told that a helicopter commonly goes out and uses the down draft from the rotor blades to blow boats clear of it. I certainly didn't want any part of that, so I steered well away.

The next afternoon saw us off Start Point with a foul tide, headwinds, and a squall bearing down on us. We were both dead on our feet and in dire need of rest. Our destination was Falmouth, still 60 NM away to the West. I took a look at the chart and found that Dartmouth was only a couple of miles away and put the helm over. We'd hold up and rest until the weather settled down a bit.

The harbour entrance was not easy to find, but it was well buoyed so we motored in between the high, tree-covered bluffs and tied up among some mooring buoys off the yacht club. I was flying our yellow "Q" flag and knew that the customs and immigrations officials would be out soon.

I stowed the sails and Ken tidied up below. By the time we had accomplished that, the customs launch came smartly alongside. We took their lines and two smiling, good-natured officers came aboard. They cleared us right away and welcomed us to England. I guess we looked like death warmed over because they told us that the new city marina had space at the dock, with showers...I guess we must have smelled dead too. We took the hint and motored to a slip in the marina. I stayed aboard but Ken checked into the hotel.

Just across the dock from us was another "Great Dane 28" named *Snow Maiden*. She was flying an American flag. I walked over and met Dick Bristol. He had the unfortunate experience of losing his rudder off Start Point the week before and was having a local boatyard build him another. Dick told me that the people who had commissioned the boat had not put a retaining block on the rudder to keep it from moving up and out of the gudgeons. In a nasty squall off Start Point the boat had pitched over a wave causing the rudder to jump up. As it came away one pintle hung up and split the rudder right down the middle and he lost it. He managed to get a tow into Dartmouth for repairs and here he sat. He was trying to get to Spain.

Dick was full of good information about what was available in town. All the best pubs and eating places, where to buy the few things we needed at the best prices. That saved us a lot of time and money. We spent an extra day in lovely Dartmouth drying out and resting up.

I enjoyed the stop over at this neat British port but I was beginning to feel a bit of urgency to keep moving. Hurricane season was progressing and time was running out. We had been delayed enough. We must move along. There was still so much to be done.

We left the Dartmouth Marina on the evening of May 18th. There was no wind so we motored around Start Point and Pawley Point. The wind finally picked up from the South giving us a beam reach. I set the main and jenny and *Blue Gipsy* was going like a train, heeling 40 degrees or more in the gusts and really romping along. Ken had to bed down in the cabin sole to get any sleep. Thus we learned that it was the best sea bunk on the ship. Being on the roll axis and wedged in between the lockers was very comfortable.

We were an hour ahead of our schedule at the Eddy stone light and two hours ahead of our E.T.A. at Falmouth. It was easy making our way into the harbour. In fact, I think it's the ideal time to get into a new harbour; just before sunrise when you can still see all the various navigational lights. There seems to be very little traffic that early in the morning too. Finally, if all else fails at least you have all day to sort it out. No doubt we had plenty to sort out.

We were both excited about being in Falmouth. This would be the place where we would outfit and provision for a trip across the Atlantic. We were also very happy to have the trials of the Baltic Sea, the Kiel Canal, the North Sea and most of the English Channel behind us. Soon we'd be out on the wide Atlantic, homeward bound...I could hardly wait....

Falmouth is a nice, well-used town with an air of history and excitement about it. Narrow streets lined shoulder to shoulder with quaint shops and stores. There is a shop for every need. Falmouth is a busy fishing and yachting center too with plenty of well-stocked ship chandlers making it easy and convenient to outfit for a voyage. Its compactness made walking to the various places quite easy. The yacht club offered coin operated showers and would handle incoming mail. It was a neat place to be.

I couldn't help but wonder how many other sailors had rode at anchor off the customs quay and stocked up for a voyage such as ours.... Many, and they are still doing it.

There was so much to buy and store aboard *Blue Gipsy*. Between forays for food and gear the "Chain Locker" pub became our favorite spot to take a break and have a pint. It is a museum of sorts too, and chock full of nautical paraphernalia, old photographs, and ships lore. A very interesting place to browse around. This is where Robin Knox-Johnston had his last beer before heading out on his solo, non-stop voyage around the world. I think Ken and I both gained a bit of confidence by savoring the history of the place...of following in the footsteps of other long distance sailors. For whatever the reason, we thoroughly enjoyed our whole experience there, but never saw Knox-Johnston.

While rowing about the harbour I came upon another bit of nautical history; the yacht "Sir Thomas Lipton," a 57 ft. ketch that Geoffrey Williams sailed to a somewhat muddled victory in the 1968 O.S.T.A.R. (Observer Single-handed Trans-Atlantic Race). I noticed that he had a set of running lights mounted on top of the mizzen mast, and thought it a good idea because they could certainly be seen at sea much better up there. It was a most interesting boat.

I became very emotional sitting there by this veteran of the sea. What a challenge, what a goal, and what a treat it would be to meet and talk with such famous men as Sir Francis Chichester, Val Howells, Blondie Hasler and David Lewis. These brave souls had started the Observer Single-handed Trans-Atlantic Race...right then and there I reaffirmed my determination to do the race the following year. But first, I needed to get this voyage completed. Then I could get involved with the O.S.T.A.R.

I rowed back to the ship and cooked a big meal. I had to get my mind back on the problems at hand. We were both famished and really enjoyed the food. Ken washed up the dishes, and then rowed the dinghy ashore to post letters and collect our mail from the yacht club. I sat quietly in the cockpit with a mug of hot tea. The sun suddenly came out and felt warm on my face. I felt the stress and strain of the years flow away. How long had it been since I had relaxed? How many years? I felt good. Here I am, I mused, aboard my own little ship in a charming English port getting ready to set off on a voyage that had been the dream of my grandfather, my father, and now me, and that dream was about to come true! I was very happy and content. My head was spinning from it all. It had been a very momentous day.

Ken came back with the mail. The mood vanished like the sun but it had been a special moment that I shall never forget. My mind turned to news from home.

My mother, bless her, always kept me well-informed about the happenings around the Island. She also encouraged me to push on with whatever it was that I was doing. Not once to this day has she ever tried to make me feel guilty or remorseful for pursuing my dreams. Her neatly typed letters would be there waiting for me when I arrived in port. I always looked forward to them and they always gave me a tremendous lift. Mail from home is so important.

We still had quite a lot to do before leaving Falmouth for Las Palmas, Canary Islands. I was running short on cash and had asked my mother to send me a draft of some sort and it had finally arrived in the mail. Eureka! That cheered me up…I immediately set about getting it cashed. No small matter in the UK. Although it was made out to me, it still had to be sent to London, then back to Falmouth before I could spend a shilling of it.

I tried not to let it spoil the day and shopped around for the things I'd buy with the money. For starters, we needed a "Walker taffrail log" to replace the very inaccurate speed/distance indicator. The Walker trails a rotor at the end of a line and as it spins in the water the clock type mechanism mounted on the stern of the ship counts the revolutions and reads out the results in nautical miles. If you read it every hour you have your speed. They are good instruments. You can haul in the line and clear the rotor when it gets fouled with weed. The only drawback is that fish like to eat the spinner.

I walked over to the local sail shop and ordered a pair of spray curtains. These fit on the lifelines on either side of the cockpit and keep a lot of spray from coming into the cockpit. I also had them paint the name of the ship on them in big black letters, so anyone could read it. Next I walked to the grocer and gave him a long list of food items that he could deliver the following day. Tinned butter, bacon, a case of eggs, cabbages, and the list went on and so did the money. We needed to be gone.

My check cleared the next day and we went about collecting the items we'd decided to purchase. The grocer pulled up to the yacht club on time and we ferried all of our supplies out to the ship. We then spent the rest of the day finding a place for it all to live. We were just in time with it too because the weather took a nasty turn.

The weather in England changes so fast it's hard to keep up with. The BBC broadcasts the shipping forecast every few hours and that is a fine service. It takes only five minutes and covers a very large area surrounding the British Isles. It seemed like a gale would roll through every few days, which kept us from accomplishing some of our chores. Not only that, it made life pretty uncomfortable.

I had been warned by other sailors in the know that the mast in the GD-28 was of airfoil shape…and that, if while at anchor the wind gets above twelve knots the mast will develop a force strong enough to heel the ship 15 degrees, at which point the ballast takes over and rolls it the other way…15 degrees. This sets up a pendulum effect, which is really awesome. I hadn't noticed it before because we'd always been in a marina or tied to a quay. But at anchor *Blue Gipsy* could swing and point her nose into the wind and that would start her to rocking and rolling and it would intensify until she would roll through 50 degrees of arc!

The first time this happened was in Falmouth. A gale swept through the area at 4 AM. Suddenly *Blue Gipsy* started to roll from side to side so hard I was almost rolled out of my bunk! After a minute or two it stopped. I thought it was only the waves from a passing boat. Just as I dozed off to sleep it started again. This was awful, we couldn't even enjoy our breakfast for the ship rolling so bad. Something had to be done. Ken and I hashed it over and decided that it was indeed the mast creating lift from the wind rushing around it. So all we had to do was disrupt the flow with a spoiler of some kind and that would put a stop to it.

We came up with the idea of running a line up the mast to act as a spoiler. So I spent a miserable hour out in the cold wind and rain playing with various pieces of rope tied to the jib halyard. The final solution was quite simple. Haul the jib sheet up to the masthead with the jib halyard, then secure each part of the sheet, one on either side of the mast as low as we could get it and pull it taut. That stopped the roll...but then the lines began slapping and clanging on the mast. Now we had a problem that not only annoyed us but everyone else within earshot. After much experimenting I finally solved that problem by hauling the halyard as taut as I could possibly get it. It was all a bit of a nuisance, but certainly worth the few minutes it took to set up. We left it in place and slept peacefully thereafter.

At last the day arrived when all was done that I thought needed doing and it was time to go. Of course the weather turned nasty and we had to delay our departure.

This was very trying on both of us. Ken seemed to get harbouritis very badly and didn't want to sail, and it was too nasty to go to town, so we sat and got on each other's nerves. (I had noticed that even in fine weather he'd come up with all sorts of reasons for not setting off, but after what I'd put him through who could blame him? Not me... but we had to get on with it.)

Finally the weather cleared and we ran up the "Blue Peter," that being the international code flag for the letter, "P." This lets all know that you are about to sail. Normally the customs and immigration people come aboard to check you out, and if all is in order, grant you permission to depart.

We waited and we waited and still no customs launch. Dick Bristol rowed up to wish us bon voyage and upon hearing our plight, vowed to track down the officials and send them over. An hour later he rowed back up and said that he'd found them in the pub and that if we didn't have any bonded stores we didn't need a clearance.

CHAPTER ELEVEN
The First Leg: Falmouth to the Canaries

DAY ONE
12:45 PM, Sunday, May 30, 1971. Falmouth, England.

A gentle breeze was blowing so I decided to get away in proper British fashion and not use the engine. I hoisted the main, took the helm and waited while Ken hauled the anchor. When he laid it on deck I put the helm over and *Blue Gipsy's* bow swung around and we were off. After stowing the anchor, Ken set about cleaning all the mud off the deck. As we quietly sailed out of Falmouth harbour I took a moment to look around one last time. Dick Bristol waved from the deck of *Snow Maiden* and we waved back and wished him good sailing. In the background Falmouth looked quite picturesque spreading out over the green rolling hills. I would miss that town and the friends we'd made. But life goes on and sailors set sail.

Ken finished his clean up and set the working jib. *Blue Gipsy* responded and we started sailing nicely. At Black Rock Buoy I trailed the Walker log, the rotor spun, and the counter began to tick off that first mile. I realized that the dream was finally coming true. The vast blue Atlantic Ocean was before us and all the years and work and toil was behind. The baton had been passed to me and all I had to do was take it on home. It should have been a good feeling but it struck a bit of sadness in my very being; it would be all over.

I shook off the melancholy mood that was trying to sneak aboard and forced my mind to dwell on the job at hand and to what lay ahead. Then a flock of gulls caught my attention. They were wheeling over a patch of water being whipped up by a large school of mackerel feeding on a school of small-fry. I handed the helm over to Ken and quickly rigged a shiny silver spoon on the rod and reel and ran the line out over the stern. I was fish hungry and this was a good chance to try our luck. In less than a minute I got a strike and set the hook. I had the fish on but we were sailing fast and it was not easy reeling it in. I heaved the fish over the rail and into a bucket Ken had dug out of the aft locker. The fish was about 18" long, a Spanish Mackerel. I took the hook out and put the line back over and caught two more in quick time and handed the rod over to Ken. I knew how much he liked to fish and just as quickly he landed two more. In about ten minutes we had landed five fish, all about the same size. We had plenty for a meal or two, so I put the tackle away and cleaned the fish. We'd have them for breakfast and lunch tomorrow.

The sun went down in a blaze of red. A good sign, "red sky at night, sailors' delight." A short while later the moon came out for a quick wink and was soon swallowed up by heavy cloud cover. It got very dark and the phosphorescence in the water was absolutely spectacular. *Blue Gipsy* looked like a star ship blasting through a coal black universe. A contrail shining a ghostly pale green streamed far astern while her bow wave rolled out a carpet of sparkling stardust. What a weirdly-lit sight it was, and suddenly we were invaded by alien beings. A school of porpoises exploded on the scene and put on a marvelous show. They would streak around like so many tinker bells, a bright ball of pulsating green light and their own contrails following along in the black depths below. There must have been a dozen of the playful creatures twisting and turning, charging toward us at breakneck speed like living torpedoes, then diving under our keel at the last possible second. The show ended all too soon and just as abruptly as they had arrived, they left and were gone and we were alone. All that could be seen was Lizard Head Light faintly blinking low on the horizon. We were finally at sea.

My watch was over at midnight, so I turned in. When I came back on deck at 0400, Lizard Head Light could no longer be seen. In fact, there was nothing to be seen except a black ocean and a cloud-covered sky. The wind had let up and we were slowing down. Around 7 o'clock the main sail gave its first "pop," and the jib screeched along the shrouds as *Blue Gipsy* rolled in the swell. I went forward and bagged the jib lest it become damaged from the chafing but left it hanked to the stay. Then I sheeted the main flat to dampen the roll and cranked the engine. I didn't want to tarry in the Bay of Biscay.

I had read that captains of the old China Tea Clippers would sail West from Lands End until they were two-hundred miles West of Cape Finisterre, Spain, then turn South. This gave them "sea room" should a sudden gale blow up. Otherwise they could get blown into the shallow Bay of Biscay with nothing but a rock-bound coast facing them. I wanted no part of that and was anxious to be past this particular area, so we motored.

DAY TWO
Monday, May 31, 1971

Ken came on deck just before 8 o'clock and I went down and started breakfast. We both like fish so I fried them up. Scrambled eggs, toast, coffee (or tea) rounded out the meal. What was left over we'd have for lunch. It had evolved that I would do all the cooking. Ken was content to wash up. I like to cook and really enjoyed the challenge. As the morning wore on the solid overcast stayed with us and prevented any work with the sextant. I was not sorry. I didn't feel very good. I wasn't sick, I just felt a little nauseated. I was also a bit apprehensive about actually navigating. Could I remember all that stuff I had learned? I was pretty confident that I could. It may take a while to work through the first sight but I'd manage. I did read up on "Consolan," which is a long-range, radio navigational aid. After lots of trial and error, I managed to get a decent "fix" which fit quite well with our DR (Dead Reckoning) position. It gave us one more tool by which to determine our position at sea.

There was plenty of animal life around and about. Little Sooty Terns, Shearwaters, Gannets, and Gulls. A few Porpoises visited but I think the engine disturbed them and they didn't stay long. There were also several ships passing through our area during the day. Apparently we were close to a shipping lane so we kept a good lookout. Ships can be sneaky and despite their size are very fast and quiet. Visibility was not more than three or four miles.

We ran the engine about ten hours that day until the barometer began a gradual slide and a nice breeze came up. I shut the engine down and raised the jenny. *Blue Gipsy* steadied and began to sail, slowly at first but the wind continued to increase and soon we were making five knots or better. We carried on through the night. The clouds blew away around midnight and the next morning we had a beautiful sunrise and the promise of a fine day.

DAY THREE
Tuesday, June 1; 47°, 41.4" North Lat. / 8°, 53.8" West Long.

We named the self-steering *Hazel* and she was developing a personality all her own, and at times it seemed as though she had a mind of her own too. For the most part she did a good job steering the ship, but I thought she could do better. The problem being, when a wave passed under the keel it threw the boat about and caused the tiller to jump from side to side. To counter this I rigged a bridle made of rubber band-like bungee cord that fit around the tiller and led over to small bronze coat hooks that I screwed down on either side of the cockpit coaming. A length of leather strap with holes punched along it allowed adjustments to be made easily and quickly. This really improved *Hazel's* steering ability and produced a much straighter course line. It also freed us up completely from baby sitting *Hazel* to make sure things didn't get out of hand. We were learning how to get the most out of *Hazel* and *Blue Gipsy* gave it her best too.

Another thing we learned about *Hazel* is that she was very powerful, and you didn't sit too close to her when the wind and seas picked up. The tiller would bump you lightly as *Hazel* cranked in corrections and then suddenly she'd give you a jab that really hurt. So other than minor adjustments for the wind or sail changes, we stayed clear of *Hazel* and let her steer the ship, which she did a great job of ninety-nine percent of the time.

By mid-morning the sun was out and brightly shining and the hour had finally arrived; it was time to start navigating. At around 9:30 I tuned the short-wave radio to WWV and started the stopwatch on the sound of the time signal. I recorded the watch's time on a note pad and handed the watch to Ken. I showed him how to write down the minutes and seconds on the stopwatch in one column, and the sextant readings that I would call out after the "Mark!" signal adjacent to them. Then, I took the Plath sextant from its fancy mahogany box and went out into the cockpit. It was not easy to get a steady stance; the boat was quite lively in the waves and heeling with the wind. It took a while before I had the sun kissing the horizon and shouted, "MARK." I took two more sights as quickly as possible and Ken copied it all down. I carefully put the sextant away and pulled out the work forms, almanac and tables.

Try as I might, the sights just wouldn't work out and didn't make any sense at all. Everything was way off, and rather than waste time with the Plath, I took my old army/navy surplus sextant out and shot a fresh series of sights. This time everything went smoothly and gave me a line of position very close to the radio and DR position. The Plath must have been knocked out of adjustment when it hit the beach at Moen. Or, perhaps, when I took it apart for cleaning. I should have had it checked in Falmouth...not a thing I should have neglected. At any rate it was a great relief to have that first line of position plotted on the chart. We both felt better just seeing it.

Just before noon, I began a half-hour-long series of sun shots to determine local noon and get a fix. Again everything worked fine and I plotted the results and put an "X" on the chart. We had a good solid fix and it was remarkably close to the various lines I had been advancing and plotting. Eureka! I could navigate. That night I used a star to sight on and zeroed the mirrors on the Plath. It proved to be a very accurate instrument even though I favored the little surplus job because it was lighter and easier to use in every way.

After the noon sight was plotted on the chart, the

First Leg: Falmouth to the Canaries

ship's log was closed out for that day and a new page started. This was a good time to have a bit of lunch. We talked it over and mutually agreed that it was a good time for the grog locker to open as well. It was also decided that one drink a day was the suitable ration. You could have a beer, gin tonic, rum, a glass of wine, or a tot of Bristol Cream Sherry. We called the sherry "granny's wine" and it became our favorite, probably because we had only one bottle.

It was remarkable how the aroma of that fine sherry would spread all over the ship when the cork was drawn and race like a flood filling my mind with fond memories of my grandfather. He had started a small winery on Daufuskie Island called "The Silver Dew Winery." He specialized in wines made from local fruit: yellow beach plums, blueberries, muscadine, scuppernong grapes, and even pears. It was what we call "sipping wine," being heavy and sweet. The aroma was as delicious and heavy as the wine. Sadly my grandfather died in the city of his birth, Charleston, South Carolina in 1968. Never would he lay eyes on *Blue Gipsy* nor hear of the voyage.

We were making excellent time with the jenny and full main. *Blue Gipsy* was obviously in her element out on the broad expanse of the Atlantic Ocean. She was a superb sea boat like her Viking ancestors.

The day wore on. There were birds in sight at all times and we noticed also a number of metal fishing floats bobbing about. I'd seen the same type floats attached to the deep-water nets of Falmouth fishing boats. Apparently they get torn off along the rocky bottoms of their fishing grounds, pop to the surface and the prevailing winds and currents sends them sailing off to the Tradewinds, and maybe all the way to San Salvador. I managed to pull one aboard with the boathook and saw a miniature nautical

world. On the submerged half of the float grew a forest of gooseneck barnacles with herds of small crabs and shrimp struggling between the gooseneck trunks. I tossed it back and cleaned up the mess.
Night came on and we started our watches. We were still sleeping on the cabin sole, the best bunk on the ship.

DAY FOUR
Wednesday, June 2; 46°, 41.8" North Lat. /10°, 15.0" West Long.

We sailed through the night and saw only the occasional ship. None came close to us.
The next morning after breakfast, I was in the cockpit staying out of Ken's way so he could clean up the galley. From out of nowhere a barn swallow flew past me and right into the cabin and tried to land on Ken's head! He was caught by surprise and let out a whoop! He had no idea what was after him. He was ducking around and beating at the bird with the tea towel. I was laughing so hard I couldn't say anything. Finally, Ken figured out that the thing was harmless and left it alone. The exhausted little bird lit on the stove railing for a rest. I crept down and caught it. Such a frail creature to be so far off shore. I forced it to drink some water, then placed it back on the stove. It preened a bit then flew out through the companionway and around the ship a time or two, then right back through the cabin and into the fo'c'sle. It perched on the rim of a locker over the v-berth, tucked its head under one slender wing and went to sleep. I still wasn't feeling too well, so put the bedding down and went to sleep too. When I awoke the bird was gone. Ken said it came out and flew off to the Northeast. I wished it luck. It was a long flight to land.
There was a confused sea running. Waves from the

First Leg: Falmouth to the Canaries 127

West riding over waves from the East were making the ship jump up and down a lot which was not very comfortable. But the water was getting noticeably warmer and the sun was getting hotter too. It felt really good to be warm and we looked forward to the trades and fine weather everyday. There were still plenty of birds about and we spent hours watching them wheeling and soaring over the waves in their endless search for food.

DAY FIVE
Thursday, June 4; 44°, 30.5" North Long. / 11°, 08" West Lat.

During the night heavy clouds moved in. The barometer, which was at 1014 millibars, started down. By 11 AM we sailed out from under the cloud but the barometer was down to 1008 millibars. Then the winds backed to the Southeast and picked up to force five. The seas followed and the barometer took a slide to 1005. It looked like we were in for a blow.

Getting the morning sun shot was a challenge. Not easy at all and by noon it was so rough I couldn't tell for certain when the sun passed our meridian. So I tuned up the DF radio and got a line off *Lugo* and *Ploneis* (Consolan stations) and capped it off with a line from the radio beacon at Cape Finisterre.

The ship by now was being hard pressed, so I went topside and reefed the main to the first batten. This eased her and helped *Hazel* to steer a better course. I changed the working jib to a number two, and although it was rough we were making excellent time in the right direction. We hunkered down and hung on. *Blue Gipsy* seemed to be enjoying the romp.

We set the ship's clocks back one hour to get things more in line with local noon. We were making our Westing and getting on down South, but we were also getting out of range of the BBC shipping forecasts. We would really miss them. From here on we would just have to take the weather as it came.

    The wind blew strong and we were sailing fast. Clouds moved in again and a light rain began to fall. I rigged our little green plastic bucket to the outer end of the boom to see if I could catch some rainwater. I also took the opportunity to wash my clothes and took a refreshing rain shower in the cockpit. The best part being when it was over; it was downright cold.

    By mid-afternoon the wind had let up and I shook out the reef and set the working jib. The wind suddenly fell light and variable, boxing the compass. I took the pole off and we adjusted the sails with every wind-change until we sailed under a cloak of dark heavy cloud. The wind came right up to near gale force and the rain was cold and fierce. I rolled the main'sl down to the second batten and again bent on the number two jib, somehow managing to lose the little green bucket. I had not noticed it when I reefed the main and apparently it had gotten torn away. We had another so it was no great loss and there was no way we could go back and find it in those conditions. It was a wild night with the seas building and beginning to break. This was our first gale at sea.

    The wind blew out of the Northeast, putting the wind on our stern quarter and that took some of the sting out of the waves. Thanks to *Hazel* we could stay in the comfort of the warm cabin and only poked our heads out to look for ships. It was really lively below and made it hard to do anything, even write up the ship's log or our journals.

DAY SIX
Friday, June 4; 12°, 42.0" North Lat. / 42°, 57.0" West Long.

"We survived the night and what a wild one it was too." So reads my journal for the beginning of this day. By mid-morning the wind was abating and by noon I had the full main up with the working jib and was thinking of putting up the jenny. But the main'sl gave its first "pop" and it was a repeat of days past. We start the engine and search for wind.

We ran the engine eight hours and finally found a breeze, very gentle out of the Northwest. I hoisted the jenny and we managed about three knots.

A school of porps came by, but I clapped my hands to see what they would do and they left us; so much for that. There are plenty of birds though and we enjoy them.

I seem to have gotten a cold. Lots of coughing, slight fever and I just felt sort of blah. I took two aspirin and felt a tad better.

The wind slowly picked up and our hopes followed. Maybe we could get some good sailing yet.

DAY EIGHT
Sunday, June 6; 40°, 10.0" North Lat. / 13°, 0.00" West Long.

We have made 133 nautical miles in the last twenty-four hours and for the last day or so we have had some of our best sailing thus far. We are also settling down to the regimen of life at sea. We are both much more relaxed and actually enjoying the trip. One reason being that it was much warmer. We are sailing almost due South and every day puts us in warmer waters and, of course, warmer air temperatures. To the East is the warm Mediterranean Sea. We feel very comfortable with the heat after being in the wet cold North for so long. Although I still have no feeling in the ends of my fingers, our bodies have healed and we just feel better all over.

We are seeing more and more flying fish, and finally the first of many came aboard; we had it for breakfast.

Our daily routine went something like this; Ken gets up around 0730-0800 and stows the bedding forward. In fine weather he'd sit out in the cockpit. I get breakfast going. When our meal is over Ken washes up the dishes, wipes down the galley, and sweeps the floor. Then we take care of personal needs, like shaving, bathing, etc. By then it's getting near time for my morning sun shot and I get everything ready for that. We warm up the radio for a time tick from WWV, check the chronometer and note its error in the log book. Using course and distance from the log I work out a DR position, then take the sights, three in a row. Ken would stay in the cabin with pencil and pad and a stopwatch. I'd take the sight and call "mark!" Ken jots down the time and altitude of the sight. When we're through, I put the sextant away and set about working out the sights. I plot all three on a plotting sheet and take the two that seem the best and plot a single line on the chart. Then I compare the results with the DR position and fret if it's too far off, and smile if it's real close. Then I put away the tools of navigation.

Next we'd work on the ship, cleaning, or repairing something, or carrying on with a project that we'd been working on the day before. Like building a better retaining rail around the bookshelf on top of the hanging locker. We had bungee cord to coral the books, but when a big wave comes along and throws the boat around the books go flying. So we replaced the cord with a teak railing and it works fine.

A half-hour before local noon I again take out the

First Leg: Falmouth to the Canaries 131

navigation tools and start a series of shots, carefully timing each one. The sun will go up, up, up, flatten out and start back down. Half way in there is high noon. When you pinpoint that, you have local noon and the height or altitude is the latitude, the time of transit is the longitude and you have a positive fix of your position. It takes about an hour from start to finish. At last the grog locker opens and we sip our ration and talk about the progress we've made, lay out new projects, or just relax. It's a nice time of the day. Then I get lunch going and we eat a light snack.

After Ken gets the galley squared away, I usually take a nap of an hour or so. My sleep at night is usually disturbed by something like a ship coming too close, or a sail not working properly or something. That nap during the afternoon helps me catch up and I enjoy it.

This brings us to the evening meal. I'd spend a lot of time and effort to prepare a good balanced meal, and to have as much fresh food as possible, like salads, coleslaw, fruit salads and the like. The main entree was a staple of rice or potatoes, with canned meats and gravies. Canned vegetables rounded off the meal. For desert we'd have fresh or canned fruit. We both loved good bread but it began to go bad in the warmer weather. On calm days I'd spread it out on the cockpit seats and dry it. Crusty bread doesn't grow mold. I'd reconstitute it by laying the slices on top of the rice when it was done cooking and the bread would become soft again. At breakfast we would use it as toast and lay on the butter and jam. We drank water or juice with our meals. If we wanted wine or beer we had to forgo them at noon. There was plenty of soda pop too.

Afterwards I'd get out of the way while Ken cleared away the galley. He'd put the kettle on and heat a pot of seawater to wash up with, Then another to rinse. Leftovers went in plastic containers and set on top of the gimbaled cooker and we'd nibble on them during our night watches.

DAY NINE
Monday, June 7; 37°, 30.0" North Lat. / 14°, 00.0" West Long.

    I had a minor confrontation with Ken this day. He had become quiet and sulky. He would let his chores slide and let me do them if I would. What brought it to a head was washing up the dishes. I didn't want to be a boss and tell him what and how to do his portion, but he was using up our fuel supply heating dishwater. I asked that he heat just enough to wash up with and then rinse with cold water. At the current consumption rate, we'd just barely make it to Las Palmas. That meant that we couldn't haul enough for the crossing. It had to be sorted out now. He argued that it was unpleasant using cold water. But I showed him our supply and how much was left. I think he was surprised at how little there was and agreed to cut back. I thought this would automatically solve the next problem, later and later galley clean up.

    I thought that by not waiting for the water to heat that he would be through with wash-up post haste, but it was not to be. He just started getting into it later and later. I had to work around dishes and pots and pans etc. It was bothersome and unnecessary. We were still keeping watch, four hours on and four hours off. I would cook when I got off at four in the afternoon. Cooking, eating and wash-up was done during his watch and I'd keep the lookout and make log entries every hour on the hour while he cleaned up. Then I'd try to lie down for an hour before I came on at 8 PM It finally got to the point that the dishes were still not done and I would have to urge him to finish up. Finally I told him that I would do the whole thing. This seemed to make him quite happy. I must say it was much easier and within 30 minutes of eating the place was squared away and gave me plenty of time to get my journal written up, take a nap or whatever before I came up on watch at 8 PM At this point Ken's sole duty was keeping his portion of the watch. I was somewhat dismayed and disappointed in this unknown trait in him. It was a side of his character I'd never seen before. But life goes on.

The warm weather brought the mold and mildew into the lower lockers. I had to take the potatoes and onions out and wash them in seawater, then wipe them with a cloth soaked in vinegar. I laid them in the cockpit floor to thoroughly dry before putting them back in the locker which had also been cleaned and wiped down. This seemed to solve the mildew problem.

The bread was going bad fast. It would not keep in plastic containers or bags at all. We'd spread it out on top of the cockpit seats, let the sun dry it and then place the slices loose in a brown paper bag. This made it last a lot longer. However, the French bread under this treatment turned into something like balsa wood and had to be sliced with a coping saw. We enjoyed it like toast.

DAY TEN
Tuesday, June 8; 35°, 40.0" North Lat. / 13°, 38.0" West Long.

My journal reads, "We've had a rough, windy night but made decent time. Plenty of heavy rain too. In the wee hours of the morning the wind veered from Southwest to West, and finally settled down out of the West-Northwest. *Blue Gipsy* took off. We have been sailing hard and fast ever since. There were several ships through our area, just enough to keep us from sacking out on watch."

After breakfast I quickly washed up the dishes and found I had an extra hour. So I took a nap. It did me good and I felt refreshed and got into the morning's navigation routine. The weather had warmed and it was time to start getting a tan. We took off our shirts and jeans and went about our chores but an hour later put them back on lest we get burned. Surprisingly we found it not all that warm. When sitting in the shade of the sail the wind actually felt cold.

We were sailing on a beam wind and I got a notion to see if I could get the ship to sail herself. I disengaged *Hazel* and set the sails this way and that. Finally I put four rolls of reefing around the boom and with the working jib sheeted in, everything balanced out and she would sail a good straight course. If I adjusted the main sheet I could alter the course a few degrees on either side of our track. I was happy with that. Should *Hazel* become damaged we would at least be able to sail some of the time without having to sit at the helm.

The day wore on and the tasks got done on time and as night fell the temperature did too. It was a cold fresh breeze blowing.

DAY ELEVEN
Wednesday, June 9; 34°, 10.0" North Lat. / 14°, 10.0" West Long.

During my watch I sewed the cover back on the logbook. The plastic was going brittle and had cracked along the seam. Then I rigged a shade around the cabin light. Every time it was turned on it would shine right in the face of the one sleeping on the cabin sole. The little kerosene lamp did not throw enough light to write by when the ship was heeling to starboard. It created a shadow as it swung and we'd have to use the overhead cabin light. The shade did the trick, and let us catch up on letter writing, ship's log and our journals without disturbing

each other.
   By mid morning the wind had let up so I shook out the reef in the main. At noon the sails gave their first "pop" and our great sailing was over. Cat and mouse time with the wind coming in little bursts from every direction just long enough to get the sails trimmed and pick up some speed, then bang! bang! bang! Nothing. We'd roll and the sails would shake the ship every few seconds. The noise would wear on our nerves too, but finally a light breeze came up from astern. I furled the main, bagged the working jib and for the first time hanked on the twin headsails. I had ordered the extra head-stay and twin jibs as a tradewinds rig. I also had two whisker poles to boom them out with. It wasn't an easy task to get it all set with the ship rolling so bad, but I finally managed. It did not dampen the roll that much, but the noise and rattling of the rigging ceased. We were also sailing along pretty well. At the end of a hour we had rolled up four knots. I felt quite pleased with myself for seeing it through.

DAY TWELVE
Thursday, June 10; 32°, 14.2" North Lat. / 14°, 54.7" West Long.

   This has been the most beautiful day of our entire trip. The sun is shining brightly, white puffball clouds blowing along on a soft, barely sailable breeze
   My Journal: "The ocean has turned from blue-green to a deep blue. It's a beautiful day."
   Off to our right, several thousand miles due West, was Daufuskie Island and home, and to our left, Safi, Morocco where Hyerdahl set off with the Ra voyages.
   I spotted a glass fishing float and since we were sailing slowly, altered course to pick it up. It was made of pale green glass with a net of heavy black cord around it.

Gooseneck barnacles covered the lower half of the float. Holding it over the side I used the kitchen knife to scrape them off. It was a nice momento of the voyage.

There were a lot of ships coming and going through our area now, apparently from the Canary Islands. One great oil tanker named *Thors Hammer* came trudging along with a huge wave at the bow. He tooted a friendly hello as we passed a quarter-of-a-mile apart. The wave turned out to be just a smooth lump in the ocean and *Blue Gipsy* climbed over it without as much as a splash.

DAY THIRTEEN
Friday, June 11; 22° C, wind Northeast force 3-4; beautiful day...

Another flying fish came aboard this morning. I didn't find him until I went to change headsails and stepped on him. Ruined my breakfast right there.

The wind went flunky at about 1000 so I took the twins off and put on working jib. We kept that until after our noon position, then the wind came up from the Northeast and our course was roughly Southwest, so up with the twins again. They are a job to set. We pulled up the log rotor and found teeth marks thereon. I guess a Dolphin took a snap at it. The sun was very hot today and I think I got a little too much so am going right to bed. We just finished our supper (rice, Irish stew, spam, tea, bread and butter), so I'm just a little sleepy too. We're rolling and banging along with following seas and wind. *Hazel* won't self steer like that. Something we've got to work on.

DAY FOURTEEN
Saturday, June 12; 28°, 31.5" North Lat. / 15°, 22.2" West Long.

No flying fish came aboard during the night because, I reckoned, neither of the mast lights would come on. The fish seemed to use that to guide their flight, hit the sails and fall on deck. I asked Ken to work on the lights and see what he could do. He found the wires corroded where they came through the deck. After cleaning and renewing the end connections they both worked fine.

I cooked up a pan of fried rice for breakfast this morning, just for a change. Although we didn't have any soy sauce or nuc-mom (Vietnamese fish sauce), it was still good.

Just after noon I was below sweating over the charts. Why couldn't we see land? Grand Canary is a high mountainous island and would be visible for many miles at sea. Was something wrong with the navigation? Had I made some dreadful error? Just then Ken let out with a loud "LAND HO!" And there, dead ahead was a great dark hunk of land. It was actually very hazy and visibility was only about 20 miles. I breathed a deep sigh of relief.

It had taken us 13 days, 2 hours and 10 minutes from Falmouth. All things considered, we had made very good time.

CHAPTER TWELVE
Las Palmas, Grand Canary

The Canary Islands are made up of two provinces of Spain; Santa Cruz de Tenerife and Las Palmas. The islands of Tenerife, La Palma, Gomera, and Hierro belong to the former, and are the Western most of the two. In fact, ancient geographers placed the edge of the world at Hierro. Las Palmas consists principally of the islands of Grand Canary, Lanzarote, and Fuerteventura. They are all volcanic in origin making them for the most part, high and mountainous.

We sailed right into the harbour of Las Palmas and dropped the anchor off the Grand Canary Yacht Club. We had the yellow "Q" flag flapping from the starboard spreader. We even cleaned up the ship and changed into clean clothes. But where were the officials?

We sat in the cockpit and watched the comings and goings of a busy port. Ships were taking on fuel at the docks. There were a lot of pleasure craft about, both sail and power, all of which were coated, we noticed, to one degree or another with heavy, black "bunker c." When a ship finished taking on this asphalt-like fuel they simply drained the hose in the harbour. What a ghastly mess.

The sun went down and I lit the Primus and started supper. If the officials showed up we'd just have to clear it away. We both got in somewhat of a plunk over being confined to the ship. Finally we turned in for the night.

The next morning dawned fair and warm. It would be

a beautiful day. I was still somewhat peeved about being ignored by the whole world. If we hadn't needed fuel and water I would have sailed right out of the filthy harbour and never looked back. But we really needed to get these important items, not to mention the mail.

Up on deck we looked around and were amazed to see a great three-legged tower right outside the harbour. It could not have been there yesterday when we came in. But how did it get there? There was a huge tug named *Swartsee* standing by and various small craft were milling about. Then it dawned on me that it was a drilling rig. We found out later they were built in Louisiana and towed across the Atlantic to the North Sea. the tug was owned and operated by the Smit company out of Rotterdam. They operate some of the biggest, most powerful tugs in the world.

While Ken inflated the Avon dinghy I collected the ship's papers, our passports, and made a list of supplies; no use wasting a row ashore.

We rowed over to the yacht club dock first and looked around for someone who spoke English, but no luck. We walked up the street to a hotel and had a talk with the desk clerk. He said that he thought it was a duty-free port and you didn't have to clear in or out. I didn't believe that but I just didn't feel up to roaming around a hot town trying to chase down someone who should have been chasing me. I was getting a bad attitude. Ken got a room in the hotel for two days. I would stay on board the ship.

We had informed our families to send the mail in care of the American Express office, but as far as anyone could tell us, there was no such thing in this town. So, I set off in search of the post office.

The buildings downtown were a mixed lot of new and old. The streets being hot and dirty. The clerk in the post office was not helpful and repeated, "no! no!" and waved his arms in the direction that we should go to get our mail. I didn't know. There was a line of people and I asked in English if anyone spoke English, but got no response. What now? Back to the hotel bar; it was time to regroup and get a better plan.

    The bartender was very friendly and sympathetic. He cheered us up with a constant stream of banter. We told him of our lack of finding the mail. "Oh," he said, "There is another post office across town, and that is probably where your mail is." We drank up and took a cab, handing the driver a slip of paper with the address. Our barman friend was very helpful.

    At the post office I handed our passports to the clerk. He looked at them, then walked over to a metal locker and fetched a big bundle of letters off the top shelf and sorted through it. We each had only one letter. We had to be missing some mail. We usually had half a dozen letters between us. Oh well, no news is good news. We posted our letters and walked back to the hotel just to stretch our legs. After a glass of nice cool beer I headed back to the ship hot and tired. I lay down and took an hour's nap and felt much better. It was late so I make a cold supper out of leftovers and warm beer. Then I wrote letters. I felt hot and sweaty so washed my hair and trimmed my beard that I had been growing since Moen. I almost shaved it off, but decided to keep it. After sundown I took a bath in the cockpit, which felt great and that cooled me off. Then I turned in. Being in a foreign country, trying to get things accomplished without speaking the language is exhausting to me. We'd have another go at it tomorrow.

    I slept well and awoke to another beautiful cool morning with a bright sun coming up. I cooked scrambled eggs on toast for breakfast. We had bought a few items at the grocery store and I was going to enjoy the fresh bread.

Las Palmas, Grand Canary

After cleaning up the ship I collected my letters, passport, etc., and prepared to go ashore. I had pulled the dinghy up on top of the cabin for the night, so I launched it and tied it to the stern railing. Next I collected all our empty water containers and one jerry jug for diesel fuel, and put it all in the dinghy. I turned around, locked up the cabin and went to get into the dinghy; it was ten feet away and moving fast! The painter had come untied. I had to do something fast. I took the letters out of my shirt, threw my wallet on the seat, kicked off my deck shoes and made a dive for the dinghy...and almost tore my front teeth out! I'd forgotten to remove the pipe from my mouth.

I managed to grab the painter and pulled the dinghy to me, climbed aboard, took up the oars, and rowed back to the ship. Well, it did cool me down. I changed clothes and managed to get ashore without further mishap. When I got to the hotel at nine o'clock Ken was still in bed, so I had to wait for him to get up. I had a funny feeling that this was not going to be a good day.

During the next two days we developed a thorough dislike for Las Palmas. It was a struggle to get anything accomplished. The people seemed to enjoy slowing us down and not giving us what we needed. Taxi drivers couldn't get you to your destination, meals were not what you ordered, and it went on and on. There was indeed an American Express office in town and we managed to retrieve our missing mail. And so it went, trudge, trudge, trudge. I was ready to go; I was tired of this place.

Finally on Wednesday, June 16 it was time to leave. I didn't have a weather forecast and I didn't really care. We were leaving.

We had to make one more trip into town for our laundry the hotel was doing, and a load of fresh bread. We got everything loaded in the dinghy and shoved off.

I was pulling away from the quay when a sharp, steep wave crashed over into the dingy; wetting our fresh cleaned and pressed clothes! Was there no end to the humiliation of this place?

Apparently not, for while we were stowing the last of the things we'd brought aboard a nearby ship took on bunker fuel, and naturally drained the hose in the harbour which made the biggest, blackest oil slick I'd ever seen. It blew down with the wind and enveloped *Blue Gipsy*, the dinghy, and the anchor line in thick goo. Oh me, oh my! We had to wait for half an hour until most of it that wasn't stuck on something, drifted away. When Ken got the anchor up we took that part of the line that was fouled and put it in the bucket and washed it with kerosene first and then soap and water before stowing it below. The dinghy had to be wiped down too before we could deflate and stow it. And finally the deck where we'd dragged the dinghy up. What a mess! Finally we raised the sails and *Blue Gipsy* moved off smartly for the mouth of the harbour, passed the huge drilling platform, and on out to sea. She seemed as eager to leave as we were. It was a relief to be gone.

CHAPTER THIRTEEN
Las Palmas to Turn-the-Chart-Over

Our relief was short lived. It was windy with lots of cloud about. Having no way to get a weather forecast we had managed once again to sail right out into the early stages of a full gale.

By the time we had everything stowed away the ship was hard pressed and needed a sail change. I went topside in my foul weather gear and reefed the main four rolls. Then I made my way forward to a heaving, pitching foredeck and bagged the working jib and hanked on the storm jib. It was slow tedious work but I managed without breaking anything or getting thrown overboard. Finally all was complete and we were much more comfortable. There seems to be no rest for the weary. It was getting late and time for our evening meal, which I was not looking forward to.

Neither of us had much of an appetite due to the rough conditions but we would not skip a hot meal just because it was rough or unpleasant. I asked Ken to babysit *Hazel* to keep the ship as steady as possible while I went down and fired up the Primus cooker. To keep it simple I made scrambled-egg-on-toast sandwiches. They were easy to handle. While I had everything going in the galley I brewed some coffee and filled a thermos for use during the night.

We both felt better after eating. It seems to settle the nerves, boost moral, and just generally improve one's outlook. I gave Ken a break at the helm for a while before laying down for a nap.

Big seas were building as the wind increased and it looked like we were in for a very rough night. I lay in the cabin sole trying to decide whether to take the mains'l off altogether or just put a deep reef in. The only problem with a reef is that the sail becomes distorted around the boom and it could damage the leech of the sail by sheeting in too hard. While these things bounced around in my head I noticed that the wind seemed to be letting up quite remarkably. About then Ken called that we were slowing down and needed more sail.

Somehow this just did not make sense. I got up and went outside. The lights of Grand Canary could be seen in the distance to windward which explained why conditions had changed so quickly…we had sailed under the lee of the lofty mountains of the island and they were blocking the wind. This was a real break for us and I quickly set about removing the working main so we could hoist the storm main in its stead.

As usual it was no easy job. With little wind and hardly any sail up *Blue Gipsy* rolled badly. The seas were building. As I lowered the working main the halyard fouled on the spreader. I seesawed the halyard and sail back and forth, up and down, and it finally came loose. I reached up to unlock the clevis from the headboard but it was gone! The quick release had let the halyard fly! At that precise instant the ship gave a lurch and I grabbed the mast with both hands to keep from being thrown overboard.

It was very dark even in the dim glow of light from Grand Canary. I heard the wayward halyard give the mast a ringing bang! What a disgusting sound on a stormy night at sea. It would just have to stay up there; I was not going to tackle that mast under those conditions.

Strong gusts of wind snatched at the mound of sailcloth as I pulled the mains'l off the mast and boom. I passed one corner to Ken and between the two of us we stuffed it down in the cockpit. Next I started to pull the storm main from its bag but changed my mind. I just didn't feel like going through it all. The storm jib would do just fine in the following wind and seas, and would be much easier to handle should we decide to heave to.

I bagged the mains'l and stowed both it and the storm main in the fo'c'sle. I had hardly gotten that done before the wind came back with a vengeance and *Blue Gipsy* took off like a young colt. I was really glad that I had used that brief calm to take the working mains'l off.

The wind and seas were steadily getting worse and thankfully both were much warmer. Not that it was warm per se, but a lot warmer than the Baltic Sea. We started short watches of two hours on and two off. I felt that in the enormous following seas we should stay out in the cockpit and help *Hazel* steer lest we get pooped and broach, or even pitch-polled. Ken openly protested.

I was not in the mood for a mutiny. I was firm when I told him that conditions would get worse, and that I was getting tired and needed rest just like he did, and furthermore, I reminded him, that standing watch was the only thing he did aboard the ship! Reason prevailed and he said, "OK" and went out in the cockpit to help *Hazel* and to keep a good lookout for shipping.

We carried on through that wild night, watch on watch. I slept like a dead man on my off-watches. Ken complained of not being able to sleep. There was nothing I could do about that and told him so. I didn't have to convince him though, of how essential our presence at the helm was. The wind had increased to full gale and the seas I estimated to be twenty-five to thirty feet high and breaking. At times we had to help *Hazel* keep *Blue Gipsy's* stern to the breaking crests of those huge seas.

I was at the helm as dawn came on. The sky cleared off but the wind was still blowing thirty to thirty-five knots, maybe more. The seas were over twenty-five feet with the bigger ones still breaking heavily. *Blue Gipsy* took it all in stride. During the night I had rigged a whisker pole to the tiny storm jib to make it behave and we were on course and going like a train. What a wild night.

It was my watch the next morning and I was sitting in the cockpit giving *Hazel* a hand, quite relaxed and content, when my reverie was interrupted by the roaring sound of a breaking wave astern like Niagara Falls. I looked over my shoulder to see a mountain of cobalt blue water bearing down on us. The log spinner was way up in the face of the wave. I watched, fascinated as it was swallowed up in a white avalanche of tumbling white water. I put the tiller under my arm and hung on tight with both hands while jamming my feet against the seats, and fought to keep the ships stern square on to the wave. And then it struck! *Blue Gipsy's* bow looked like it was pointing straight down and I wondered if we would be pitch-poled end over end. But we weren't. The wave crashed all around and on top of me. And then it was gone. Water was cascading off the decks and the cockpit was full to within inches of the seat tops! I quickly got out our trusty bucket and bailed as fast as I could. I could feel the weight of the water pressing *Blue Gipsy* down. Another wave like that one and we could be in real trouble. Between the cockpit drains and the bucket, the water was quickly removed. Ken popped his head out to see what had happened. I assured him that everything was OK and he went back to his bunk.

That had been a close call. I took stock to see if *Hazel* was damaged and noticed the log line wrapped around the wind vane and twisting itself into a knotty mess. Simply amazing I thought; how something so fragile could come through that crash of water without being torn to pieces.

Everything seemed OK, so I set about pulling in the log rotor and unwinding the line. It took a while but I finally had it sorted out and working properly. Ken came out and I turned the helm over to him and went down to start breakfast. I was tired and hungry.

I heated up two cans of soup for breakfast. I felt that would warm us up and give us a shot of quick energy. Hot mugs of tea followed and we both enjoyed it. After wash-up I told Ken to go down and get some sleep. He looked exhausted and lost no time in getting below snuggled down in his sleeping bag and was soon sound asleep. He had apparently gotten over his sleeping problem. I let him sleep. He got up once or twice to look around but went back to bed. I got him up at 1200. Enough was enough. The rest did him good though and he did look much better for it.

I got busy and just managed to get everything ready for the noon sight. Although it was still quite rough I took my time and got a good series of sun shots with which to work out our noon position. The plotted position showed that in spite of the heavy weather and reduced sail we had made good time.

The wind and seas had abated a little by the time I put everything away, so we took our lunch and grog break. By the time that was done we needed to get more sail up and get moving. But first I wanted to get the loose halyard down. We talked it over and agreed that climbing the mast was out of the question. The ship was rolling too badly. Ken suggested using a sinker with the spinning reel to toss a line over the halyard; which at the moment was stretched taut between the mast and the aft stay.

I would try anything to keep from climbing up that gyrating mast. It seemed worth a try, so I dug out the little spinning rod and reel. Then I tied a small lead sinker to the end of the line. After a few practice throws to get the feel of it, I flipped the sinker over the halyard and pulled the line taut. The sinker obediently wrapped itself firmly around the wire and while I kept pressure on the line Ken shook the halyard loose. I maneuvered the line around and around the mast and rigging and finally had the halyard in my hand. I asked Ken to fetch the hacksaw so I could remove the fitting from the cable. I had no intention of allowing that particular fitting to put us in peril again. While Ken was rummaging around in the tool drawer the ship gave a sudden roll and the halyard was whipped out of my hand! I couldn't believe my eyes! I should have been on guard because things had gone too smoothly. I watched as the halyard swung out over the water, the ship rolled back, the halyard stopped in mid air and then started its return swing toward the ship…right for me. I stuck my hand out and made a perfect catch! I had it again! I took a death hold on that halyard and didn't relax my grip until we had sawed off the quick release fitting and installed a deep clevis with a threaded pin. Then I secured the halyard to a ring in the mast.

I decided to hold off on setting the mains'l for a while…it was still blowing pretty hard and the waves were still very high. We did, however, need more sail up and opted for a number two jib, one of the twin downwind jibs, actually. I went forward and lowered the storm jib but left it hanked on the port forestay in a bag lashed to the pulpit. I set the number two, rigged the whisker pole and its preventer, then went back to the cockpit to see how *Blue*

Gipsy would handle the change. She seemed delighted and really moved out. In less that a heartbeat a strong gust of wind hit the sail and tore the clew right off about six inches above the "D" ring. I dashed forward but by the time I had the sail down the cloth was frayed at the tear. Now I was faced with a major sail repair. So much for adding sail too early in heavy weather. I hoisted the storm jib again and we carried on.

The wind and seas went down within the hour and I ventured out and bent on the working main, reefed it four rolls, then set the other number two jib. We started sailing really fast. It was turning into a beautiful day after all.

And so, our first heavy gale at sea was over. All things considered we had come through in pretty good shape.

Sunday, June 20; 23°, 44" North Lat. / 23°, 13.7" West Long.

We were making good time, 134 nautical miles in the past twenty-four hours. We were still heading a bit South of West to get down into the trades. We would swing to a more Westerly course in the next day or two. Twenty degrees North should be far enough South to stay in the trade wind belt. We had now picked up a knot or two of current, which would give us a needed boost of twenty to thirty miles per day. We felt like we were on the right track and really headed for the barn.

I tried to get Ken interested in navigation but no luck. The wind seemed to have gone out of his adventurous sails. He showed little interest in anything actually...even taking a bath, and I had to ask him to do that. He was getting randy and the water was delightfully refreshing in the middle of the day. I'd use our bucket to bring seawater up and pour it over my head in the cockpit. Then soap up and a draw a few more buckets to rinse, followed by a good brisk rub down with a towel. That was the secret of not feeling sticky after a saltwater bath...the rub down.

We sorted through our apples and oranges and had to throw a couple of each away. That was sad to me for we both enjoyed them very much. One of each per day was our ration and we had quite a few extras. I vowed to go through them daily and catch the ones going off and eat them up rather than throw them away.

I noticed the white plastic jug of water tied in the corner of the cockpit was turning a light shade of green. I smelled it and it seem all right. I read the label on the Clorox jug, under "water purification," gave the container the prescribed dose and hoped for a cure. Meanwhile I started cooking with it so we wouldn't loose it should it go completely off. We had a long way to go and I did not want to run out of water.

That torn sail was heavy on my mind and I was trying to come up with a fix. I searched for the sail repair kit but couldn't locate it. I finally found some strong sail thread and a couple of rusty needles in the bottom of my locker. I had no extra sail cloth so used the back of a flotation cushion. It was a strong white vinyl of sorts that should hold up all right. After the noon sight and lunch I set to work and at the end of two hours I was hot and flustered. I'd cut a neat incision in my thumb with the rigging knife and broke one of my needles, but I had a repair that would hold up until we arrived in port, if we took it easy on the sail.

We had settled down a bit now and were more familiar with how the ship was performing. We were also much more confident at her ability to carry sail and to realize just how tough she was. For example, in the mornings the wind would increase as the sun came over the horizon. Lots of cloud would be generated then too. But the increase in wind-strength would upset *Hazel's* tender hand on the helm and she would tend to broach the ship at the bottom of the wave. This at times caused a jibe of either the main or jib and would stop us cold if not taken care of before it was carried too far. To counter this maneuver without having to scramble up through the companionway and into the cockpit, I rigged a light line from the wind vane itself, through an eye on the pushpit railing, led it along the cockpit and below. Now when *Hazel* lost it, all we had to do was pull on the line and viola! The ship came back on course. This was a real boon to the one on watch.

The next morning I went forward to change the headsail from the number two to the working jib. I didn't notice that the forehatch had a thin coating of white sea salt on it, and when I stepped on it my foot slipped and I went down. My right knee landed right on the jib sheet that was draped across the hatch. I didn't think much about it. It hurt but was not overly painful. A short time later I had what looked like half a goose egg under the skin of my knee, and it was impossible to bend my leg over half way. Indeed, I could just barely manage to go up and down the companionway.

This really concerned me. Not so much the pain and discomfort but the seriousness of a possible complication with an injury of that kind. I could have, and probably did have, a fractured kneecap. I had to wonder; could Ken handle the ship should things get out of hand? I tried not to dwell on the possibilities for they were all rather grim.

The next day my knee was swollen but not overly sore or painful, it just looked so bad. The area around the goose egg was red and quite tender when pressed. There was a lot of fluid trapped inside. I really wondered if we might have to do surgery on it to relieve the pressure. I decided to put some cool, seawater compresses on it for an hour or so to see if it would go down. It didn't. I vowed to go easy and not bother the thing and maybe it would eventually just go away.

By now we were getting into mid-ocean and out of range of regular radio, including the powerful BBC. I began using the short-wave bans to pull in WWV in Ft. Collins, Colorado for time ticks so I could check the rate of gain or loss on the ship's chronometer. I'd bought it from Baess and screwed it down to the tabletop. It was keeping excellent time and I liked to wind that impressive piece of equipment every day. It would be our navigational timepiece should the Zenith trans-oceanic radio pack up. It had had a rough voyage thus far and I wasn't sure how much water had gotten into the innards of the thing. Ken kept an Acutron wrist watch in his locker which also kept good time, but there again it was running on a small battery that could go dead. The ship's chronometer gave us both an edge of confidence that we would be able to navigate and find our longitude should all else fail.

With the exception of flying fish and birds, all other animal life had disappeared. We were a thousand miles from Grand Canary. Only one little British Storm Petrel seemed to linger along with us. The flying fish were in abundance and several would come aboard each night. These we collected, cleaned and added to the breakfast menu. The outside air and the seawater temperature were much warmer now. Each morning there was heavy dew all over the topsides of *Blue Gipsy*. I thought it might be a source of emergency drinking water if sopped up with a cloth and wrung out into a container. I tried it but it was saltier than the sea. In fact it was sea salt dissolved with a bit of dew.

My knee was improving and the swelling continued to go down. I was much relieved and continued to be careful with it as much as possible.

It was time to try the twin down-wind jibs. I spent some time getting the longer tack wires installed on the stem fitting, hanking on the jibs, and rigging their sheets and whisker poles; at last we hoisted them both up. Each sail had its own stay and each its own halyard. Then I furled the main and secured it on the boom and put the sail cover on.

What a disappointment. The ship rolled through fifty degrees of arc and we certainly didn't go any faster. I decided to hang on to them for a while and try to improve things by changing our heading a few degrees or the like. But nothing would make them do what I envisioned. In fact, if I sailed due West on course, the starboard jib would be backed with almost every roll. In disgust I took it off and hoisted the main and we were able to sail our course with only half the roll and a full knot faster. So much for my plans.

Another thing I got into was reducing sail at night. With a jib on a whisker pole and the main reefed down to the first batten, we made excellent time and *Hazel* was able to hold a much better course without so much thrashing about. We were learning and this made the voyage much more relaxing. I was thoroughly enjoying myself and was sorry for Ken because he was only looking forward to the end of the voyage. I was looking forward to many, many more miles in *Blue Gipsy*.

On June 25 the weather changed to a cloudy mackerel sky and the wind began to let up somewhat. Our speed dropped to four-and-a-half knots and we were a bit concerned about a tropical wave coming through. We did not need a storm or the beginning of a hurricane. Then a cold front approached from the East, collided with the warm damp air that was over us, and it began to rain. That night it cleared off and we had dry decks and one of the most beautiful starry nights I have ever seen; it was just beautiful. I sat in the cockpit and steered for a couple of hours, and even got a kink in my neck from just gazing up at that spectacular star strewn sky. It was worth it.

The next day the winds came on strong and we once again were rolling along...literally. I had the twin jibs hanked on and pulling, but it really got tiresome. I was glad when the wind backed to its normal Northeast and we could put the mains'l up again. By tacking slightly it steadied the ship considerably, but gave *Hazel* a fit.

There was a lot more Sargasso weed about, and we saw our first delicate looking white tropic bird and a lesser shearwater (a bullet-shaped bird of medium size, but could they ever fly down the face of the waves, wheeling and turning as they caught the currents of air a foot above the face of the wave). I rigged a rod and reel with a feathered lure and hoped for a Dorado, but didn't have much luck.

June 27; 20°, 14" North Lat. / 40°, 40" West Long.

We saw our first ship in nine days. I had gone out in the cockpit to have a look about just after lunch and there, about a mile behind us was a great white ship. She came up along our port side rather quickly and slowed to about ten knots only about a hundred feet away. It was the motor vessel *Leon-puerto Cortez*, A South American banana carrier. A big blue seal with the name *Chiquita* painted on her side. The crew was lined up along the rail and seemed a happy, friendly lot, smiling and waving. Using a loud hailer the captain asked, "Do you need anything? Cigarettes—Coffee?" "No thank you!" we shouted back. Coffee we had and neither of us smoked cigarettes. (I puffed on a pipe.) Then he called over his latest position, which I jotted down on a note pad. Then the propeller increased its tempo and they started to pull away. One last question; "Where are you bound?" "San Salvador!" we replied. A final wave from all hands and they were gone.

We were somewhat refreshed from the excitement of having a full-grown ship right there next door and chatting with the captain. It made us feel good to know that there were other people in our watery world. I felt even better when I checked his position with mine and they were very close.

We rolled along under the tug of the twins which made life sort of hectic. It was not easy to do anything with the ship rolling so much. It was so bad it wore the gimbals out on the stove and one end fell on the counter top! I riveted a piece of phenolic sheeting across the gap and that acted as a bearing surface and it worked fine. With that in mind I checked the kerosene lamp and saw the holes were elongated in it. I rotated the gimble 180 degrees to give it some new meat and put a drop of oil on the pin. That would help keep the wear down.

June 26; 20°, 03.1" North Lat. / 42°, 59.7" West Long.

FROM MY JOURNAL:

Today ladies and gentlemen is TURN THE CHART OVER DAY! *(clapping from the crowd—a real earth-shaking ovation with much hullabaloo—cat-calls and a fist fight on the fifth row back.) Yes friends, after only thirteen days and 1600 miles we have finally arrived at that great divide, that crease in the chart at 41°, 25" West Longitude. Today we get on the same side of the chart as the real world...a little screwed up perhaps but the real world nonetheless. Ah, the life of a sailorman, full of stirring events.*

After I had plotted our position and with great fanfare, I flipped the chart over. I could almost hear the people in Ken's head roar their approval of the good news.

My, how clean and nice the new side was. Hardly a blemish. Well I mused, the first half had certainly been interesting; wonder what the next half will bring?

Yes, we had muddled through it all and knew now that we had a lot more skill and confidence; we were more seasoned, and a whole lot more experienced. I felt we could handle the flip side of the chart a lot better, but time would tell.

CHAPTER FOURTEEN
The Cradle of the Deep

The varnish was beginning to show signs of hard use so I asked Ken to sand it all down and brush on a fresh coat. He jumped right on it. I was surprised at his sudden show of enthusiasm. Maybe he thought that we would reach the other side of the ocean after all. Not to pass up such potential, I hit him again with the idea of learning how to navigate and he agreed!

The next morning I shot the usual set of sights with the little air force sextant then handed the instrument to Ken to let him try his hand. It was a slow, tedious process. After much coaxing and encouragement he had three sights in a row that he thought were OK. We went below and I talked him through the procedure for reducing them and then we plotted both series on the chart. He was quite pleased with himself; his line of position was within five miles of mine. I was pleased to see the change in him. It would take some time for him to become proficient, but at least he knew that he was capable of doing it.

After we were through with all that I went topside to see what I could do with the sails. I kept working with various headsails not willing to admit how awful the twins were. I even poled the jenny out to see if it would keep the roll down but only managed to pull the "D" ring off the clew of the sail. Another sail repair. I had finally found the sail repair kit so had no problem re-attaching it. We had learned through trial and error that even with the rolling, *Hazel* could steer the twins a lot better than any combination of sails including the mains'l. With the mains'l up, the ship kept trying to round up into the wind. To help *Hazel* counter this we finally developed an improved harness for *Hazel*. We used a pair of bungee cords, one on either side of the tiller, to give *Hazel* scope to steer, but with a rope limiter built in so she could only correct a set amount. Otherwise in a day or so of oversteering she simply tore the bungee to pieces and ran all over the ocean. We were learning how to cope with all the variables, and could change our technique for the situation at hand. Our daily runs were averaging 125 to 130 nautical miles. I vowed to keep working with the headsails.

I love to fish and usually had a lure of some kind trailing over the stern. I used a 4/0 reel and a short, stout rod full of 40 lb. test mono. It was somewhat of a nuisance though. The lure was constantly picking up sargasso weed and we'd have to reel it in to clear the hooks. But we were determined to catch something. Finally one night the reel let out a scream as line peeled off the spool into the inky blackness astern. I ran out in the cockpit, unlatched *Hazel* and shoved the tiller over and hooked it behind the cockpit coaming. *Blue Gipsy* rounded up into the wind, backed the jib and stopped. After a short fight I hoisted in one of the most extraordinary fish I had ever seen. The hapless creature was snagged in the tail. It was the color of a Mackerel but looked like a foot-long Barracuda that had been stretched to three feet. It had enormous eyes and a formidable set of teeth. I remembered seeing a picture of a fish just like that

Departing Las Palmas

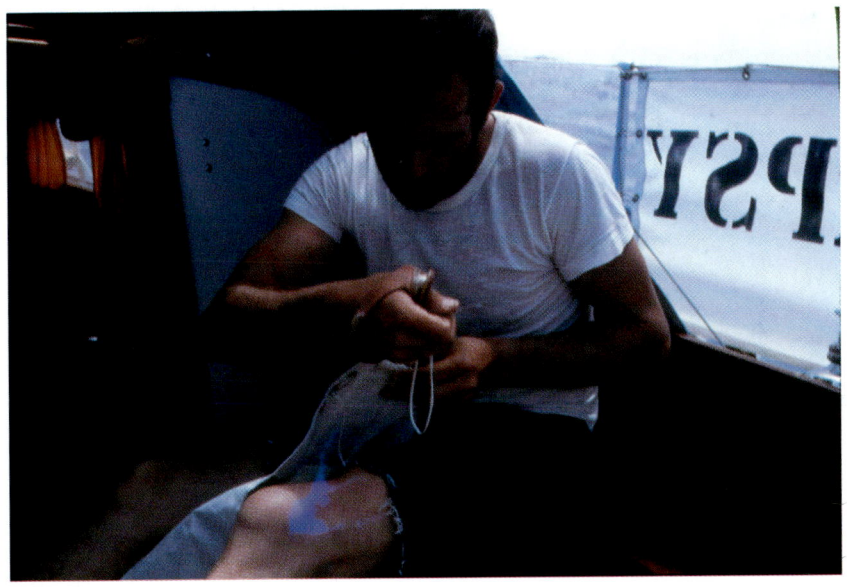

Repairing sail

Plath sextant

Strong tradewinds and seas

Walker Log

Hazel steering the ship

Drying and sorting the potatoes

Sunrise in the Trades

Dolphins visit

White tropic bird

Sargasso Weed

Bent boom

Ken and Blue Gipsy

Chiquita Banana boat

Savannah friends

Home at Last…

recently…and sure enough when I looked in my copy of Hyerdal's classic book, *Kontiki*, there it was. They identified it as a Snake Mackerel. Apparently they were the first people to ever catch and record one alive. After a thorough examination we cleaned it and the next morning I fried it up for breakfast. It was not that good and I could never imagine a fish with such bones. The thing was essentially a basket made of bones with a bit of meat here and there and a skin stretched over it to make it look, more or less, like a fish. We decided that it was not worth the fuss and bother and would not keep another one should we land it.

One night the moon arose full, sharp, and clear. It was a beautiful sight. It had been a long time since I had shot the moon for a line of position. So, just to keep up on things I took the sextant out and shot a quick set of three sights. Ken grumbled a bit but wrote down the time and altitude when I called "mark!" Then I patiently reduced them and plotted the results on the chart. The line came in quite nicely with our advanced noon position.

The moon, I personally feel, is hardly worth the effort to use for navigation on a regular basis. It wasn't that easy to bring down and there are too many corrections to muddle through. It would be fine if you haven't had a chance to navigate for a day or so, or maybe when making a landfall at night. That's why I did it, just to prove to my own satisfaction that if I needed to, I could.

I had tried to use stars at sea too, but found them too difficult to bring down. Conditions had to be perfect and even then it was not easy. Poor visibility made it hard to tell when they were on the horizon. The sun, on the other hand, is big, fat and bright. The horizon is easy to see and even the computation is relatively straight forward. I decided to stick with old sol.

The Sargasso weed was getting thicker and broad rafts

and windrows of the tough, golden-yellow weed were everywhere. It looked like a solid mass but was really just small clumps that drift together. It didn't seem to slow us down as we sailed through the thickest of it. I used our boathook to pick up several wads and shook them in a bucket on the foredeck. Soon I had the most interesting collection of miniature shrimp, crabs, snails and fish we had ever seen. Many were designed especially for life in the Sargasso, and indeed they looked like the weed itself. A fascinating collection to say the least and this became one of my favorite pastimes and I never tired of the variety of animals that showed up in that bucket.

There were numerous Portuguese man-o-war about and we had to be very careful about bringing water up in the bucket for our baths. That would make life miserable indeed if one managed to deposit a slippery, stinging tentacle down ones back or some other tender spot. On more than one occasion when we pulled the log line in to clear away the weed a bit of the stinging mechanism would touch the back of a finger or hand like a red hot branding iron and we'd have to get out the household ammonia to doctor it. I had bought it in Falmouth specifically for that purpose and was glad we had it aboard as an antidote.

We lost our fishing lure. Either the Sargasso weed fouled the lure and broke the line or a big fish ate it. At any rate it was gone and it was the only one I had so decided to make a replacement. I used a hefty hook and bits of white cloth to tie a big "fly." I hoped it would look like a small flying fish to a Dorado. I put this out and it worked great merrily bouncing over the surface of the water and didn't get caught in the Sargasso nearly as much as the deep running lure did. I knew it would work fine and that eventually we'd get a nice fish, that was good to eat.

JOURNAL ENTRY, July 1, 1971

> *The only bird life now is a solitary white tropic bird. It's with us everyday, flying along in its ungraceful way. The bird seems to always be trying to make up its mind to land on something. I've never seen it dive, although I have seen it sitting on the surface of the water, paddling around, its long tail feathers held high so they don't get wet. I wonder how it feeds, and on what? It is obviously a strong flyer, it just looks so uncoordinated.*

We spent a lot of time watching this and other birds and really enjoyed their company. I almost felt that they enjoyed ours too.

On July 2, we sailed our fastest day, 141 nautical miles in twenty-four hours with the full main out to port and the jenny poled out to starboard, wing and wing. That night, on my watch, the snap shackle on the jenny pulled apart and before I could get it down the broken piece beat a few small holes in the clew of the sail. I replaced the fitting and reset the sail. I could repair it later. Ken, aroused by all the noise, came out and handled the sheets. All went well and we were quickly back under full sail and at full speed and Ken went back to bed. I was so comfortable with the ship and the way she sailed that if we'd have had a spinnaker on board I would have put it up too. At times I wished for twin genoas, I'd have flown both of them but, maybe it's just as well that I didn't for there's no telling what might have happened.

Just at dawn a squall came through with a lot of heavy black cloud. I didn't want to get Ken out to help me reduce sail so I just hung on and helped *Hazel* steer. That was a mistake. It finally got so bad that something had to be done. Reluctantly I called Ken and while he handled the sheets and watched the helm I took the jenny off, reefed the main to the second batten and then raised one of the twins as a number two jib. The barometer was falling fast and was down to 1007 millibar. I was very concerned about a hurricane forming. We were right in the middle of the season and the area where they spawn. I prayed that it was just a local disturbance, or a weak tropical wave and carried on.

I kept tapping the glass and every time it dropped even lower. Finally I decided that the instrument was packing up, and sure enough it was. That took care of that, at least we wouldn't have to keep banging on it anymore. The heavy weather seemed to follow us along giving some hard, fast sailing.

The next morning I smelled something rotten aboard the ship and went through each locker giving it the old sniff check. I finally found a potato that had gone off. I cleaned out the locker and washed it down with seawater and vinegar. Then I carefully repacked it. I was surprised at how well the food kept in the heat of the tropics.

During the search I found an apple under the dinette; it had fallen behind the dinghy. EUREKA! This was a real treat. I carefully and precisely cut it exactly in half. The taste was fantastic and we savored every morsel. We had been out of apples for several days now and sorely missed them. Sad to say the oranges would be gone next. We were running out of fresh fruit.

July 6; 21°, 53" North Lat. / 59°, 54.4" West Long.

JOURNAL ENTRY...

Radio Antilles reports that there is a depression to the Southwest of us and moving off toward Cuba and a tropical wave is moving in from the East. That is the system that we are in at the moment, and explains why it was so cloudy and rough. I'll be glad when it gets back to sunny skies and puffball clouds.

July 7...

    Well, I blew it last night. I came down to fill out the log book when a large wave hit the ship and slew her around. I dove for the tiller but the mains'l jibed over with a bang! That dinky boomvang tackle with the key slot under the boom is a laugh. The line twisted out of the camcleat on the fiddle block and allowed the boom to swing amidships before it was brought up abruptly by the stop knot in the end of the line. This put an enormous strain on the center of the boom, the boom bent, which caused it to crack and now the outer end of the boom is deflected up about two feet. At the same time the snapshackle on the number two jib pulled apart and the sail started flogging like crazy. That was the last el cheapo, brand-X snap shackle.
    I put the helm over to keep the boom where it was and called Ken. I was afraid to jibe it back lest it break the boom completely in half. He came out and steered on a downwind tack while I lowered the jib and put on a new snap shackle. Now, like the jenny, there are several small holes in the clew of this sail. I reset the jib, then lowered the mains'l and took it off the mast and boom. Thankfully the boltrope slipped through the bent part of the boom without undue difficulty and left the sail undamaged. Now I really had a problem; how was I going to fix this boom?

    We carried on through the night under reduced sail. I just didn't want to put up another headsail in the rough conditions we were experiencing. Besides I'd had about as much excitement as I could stand for one night. I turned the watch over to Ken and went below to my bunk.

It was relatively quiet and peaceful below, lying on the deep pile of sleeping bags and blankets. If felt good to rest and calm down. I was not sleepy; the adrenaline from all the action had not worn off. That had been quite a workout with the mains'l and jib. My mind raced ahead as to what to do. First, lay out the problem.

1. The boom was bent and cracked.
2. Was the boom strong enough to be used like it was?
3. Could it be straightened? Maybe saw it in half at the break and put a plug inside, then slip it back together? What kind of plug?
4. Maybe get it welded in San Salvador? (I seriously doubted that).
5. Perhaps we should change our destination to Nassau. Certainly they would have a shop capable of such a repair, or even a replacement boom?
6. I may be able to rig a tackle to bend the boom back the other way and straighten it...

My mind was still mulling over all the variables when I finally fell asleep.

All too soon Ken was calling me out for my watch at 4 AM. I felt refreshed and alert from the good sleep. The motion of the ship under reduced sail was much easier and no other emergencies had cropped up to awaken me. The wind had moderated somewhat and that helped.

In my mind I continued to map out a plan of attack on the busted boom. It went like this; first off, I would only try to straighten the boom; not cut it and insert a plug. Obviously it was still quite strong and besides, I didn't have anything readily available to make a plug from. And secondly, we should head for Nassau rather than San Salvador. There we would have a much better chance of a quality repair or replacement.

The next morning, after breakfast and wash-up I got to work on phase one; the boom itself.

To start with, I used the roller-reefing handle to rotate the boom 180 degrees. This positioned the damaged area to the topside of the boom. Then I rigged a heavier double-block and tackle to the jib track. Next I used a loop of nylon webbing to wrap around the boom so that it had a wrap going on either side of the break. Then I hauled the boomvang tackle taut. This put a strain on the boom to straighten it. I pulled it as taut as I dared without pulling the track out of the deck or breaking the topping lift. Then I took a small ballpeen hammer and peened the area opposite the break. This helped stretch the metal and the boom slowly straightened. Finally there was only about a 6-inch deflection at the outer end of the boom. I could live with that.

I carefully bent on the mains'l and hoisted it. It really didn't look as bad as I thought it would. A bit sloppy on the leech, but after adjusting the leechline it looked fine. The boom was strong enough to take the strain and *Blue Gipsy* responded to the increased sail and we picked up speed. I laid out a new course and we were Nassau bound.

July 8; 22°, 52.2" North Lat. / 64°, 40.0" West Long.

JOURNAL ENTRY...

The weather continues to be more or less good, but with scattered rain squalls. They are small and you can see them coming from miles away. So far we have not had to reduce sail...we keep our fingers crossed. But the weather is really unstable, and so it should be; this is the hurricane season. In fact, the first tropical storm of the season has formed North of us, and is heading off to the Northeast. It offers no threat, but it does make one aware of the possibility of danger. I know now why I pushed so hard to get through this particular part of the ocean. I'll be happy to see it behind us. It will continue to get worse and even more unstable. It will also get hot, humid and steamy.

Right now we're banging along in light air, at four-and-a-half knots. The jenny gives a loud "POP!" when we roll extra hard. A look at the pilot chart shows that this area experiences eight percent calms and light airs compared to only four percent for other areas around it...strange but true.

Our white tropic bird is a dummy. It came around this morning checking us over. Not satisfied with that, it tried to land on the starboard spreader for a better view. Naturally when he got close, the ship rolled and the mast swatted it. There was a loud BONK! And a frantic beating of wings as the bird flew off, shaking its head. It's lucky to be alive.

The one bird now over the horizon, and the ever-present flying fish are the only animal life to be seen. There are still tons of Sargasso weed about.

July 9; 23°, 24.1" North Lat. / 66°, 54.8" West Long.

JOURNAL ENTRY...

We have had two days of light winds but have thus far still managed our one hundred or more miles per day. As long as we drop no lower than this, I am content. If we

do I'll still have to be content...but not enjoy it.
I got quite a shock this morning. I noticed that the carpet on the cabin sole was damp and I suspected the fresh water pump was leaking and running down. I asked Ken to have a look. When he checked it out, he found the bilge full of water! We cleared it right away with the pump and after a frantic search found the stuffing box around the prop shaft leaking a steady stream of water. We had forgotten to give it a squirt of grease the last time we ran the engine. Now we have a new rule; the bilges will be cleared each morning and evening. We also must remember to grease the stuffing box after we are through charging the batteries and shut the engine down. That should take care of that.

Just at noon a huge rain squall came upon us from astern. I was in the process of taking the noon sight, and just barely got it but all our bedding and some clothes we'd washed was draped all over the rigging. We had tied it with small line to keep it from getting blown overboard. Well we couldn't just stop everything at that crucial moment so carried on. By the time we finished up with that, a curtain of heavy rain was right behind us. We scurried about trying to untie stubborn knots and shove stuff down the companionway or through the forehatch. We made it though. With everything safely below I had Ken stand by the jib halyard should we need to drop the jenny. Sometimes these squalls have a lot of wind in them. We both stayed out in the rain. It felt cold and refreshing after the hot muggy weather we had been having lately. There was not much wind and no lightening, just heavy rain. It moved off to the West and rained itself out. But it took the wind with it and left us flapping and banging in the heavy swell. We are becalmed. Not to pass up an opportunity I donned mask, fins and snorkel and after throwing a safety line over the stern, jumped overboard. There's nothing like a refreshing swim and a look around the ship.

The first thing that caught my eye was a gob of monofiliment fishing line wrapped around the electronic log propeller. That is what had stopped it. I had Ken hand me a knife and I cut the line off and cleared it away. Next, there were a few patches of gooseneck barnacles at the turn of the bilge. I handed up the knife and asked for the spatula and used it to clean them off. While I was at it I also cleaned the prop real good. Finally I checked the rudder pintles and gudgeons. Everything seemed to be in good shape.

I really wanted some pictures of Blue Gipsy's pretty bottom so I traded the spatula for the Nikonos underwater camera and took a dozen pictures from various angles...it gave one a real fish-eye view of the ship.

I tried to get Ken to go for a swim but he would have nothing to do with that. I guess the idea of the water being several miles deep and full of big, hungry animals was too much for him. But I enjoyed myself and was happy that I had the chance to experience such varied sensations. It was not easy to swim away from the ship. The fact being that there are a lot of big hungry animals out there. The water is several miles deep and to be separated from one's life support system was awesome, like being born and severing the umbilical cord. None of these things stopped me but those survival genes were screaming.

CHAPTER FIFTEEN
Bahamas Landfall

July 10, 1971; 23°, 55.8" North Lat. / 69°, 02.6" West Long.

JOURNAL ENTRY...

The day's sailing can be best described as light and noisy. At 0630 we were becalmed. The ship was rolling heavily and the sails were slatting and banging around. The jenny was killing itself against the port spreader and the radar reflector. Finally, I couldn't take it anymore and took the jenny down, left it rolled along the deck, went below and went to sleep in the quarterberth.

I popped out at 0900 to find the twin I had left up had backed in a nice, East-Southeast breeze of five to six knots. It had stopped our rolling...That's why we slept so good.

We both got up. I went forward and hoisted the jenny but was unable to sail our course without backing the jenny. I had nailed things down so well with preventers that it was no small matter to change over to a port tack, but there was nothing else to do, so I got with it.

It took a while to swap the headsails around, then get the whisker poles rigged and secured. Our speed picked up to three-and-a-half to four knots, so the change had paid off. Just when things settled down I noticed a rainsquall passing us on the downwind side and suddenly the wind backed around to the Northeast, which backed the jenny again! I was determined not to go through a repeat of the earlier changeover, so I set Hazel *and let her steer. It turned out to be a smart move because as the rain squall moved off, the wind slowly came back to East-Southeast and we sailed on course for the Bahamas.*

A second white tropic bird showed up and it was quite entertaining to watch their antics. Both were fascinated with the log rotor and flew for miles swooping down close to the water but pulling back short of hitting the surface. They would also take turns trying to land on the mast head, but never quite got it together and only succeeded in getting swatted a couple of times. They are tough birds though and survived these encounters without apparent damage to themselves.

I finally saw them dive for a fish but due to the wave action never managed to see what they caught. Tiny flying fish I would assume—they were the only plenteous fish around.

Ken continued to improve with his navigation and I let him take the sights and work them out and plot them. I would follow behind him, check over his worksheets and the plot. We discussed and corrected any errors and he learned how to navigate, and that made us both feel better. I could tell that he was quite pleased by the fact.

Our meals were getting quick and simple. The oppressive heat made cooking an ordeal, so the can opener worked double time. Salmon salads, crackers and dip, canned fruit desserts and the like. When I did boil potatoes I'd cook a lot, and have the extras in a salad for the next meal. Ken didn't complain. Both of us longed for a fresh fish.

We enjoyed listening to the radio. We'd keep up on the news from the BBC and Radio Antilles. We also continued to get time hacks and weather blurbs from WWV. But the announcers, I'm convinced, were hired with speech impediments and a love for chewing gum. It was impossible to hear over half of what they said. No great loss while within range of a reliable station, but frustrating to the limit when that was all we had.

The temperature in the cabin was over ninety degrees Fahrenheit every day now. The cockpit seats were hot enough to blister bare feet. There was not a cool place on the ship except when you could find some shade under a sail. I rigged a plastic survival blanket over the cockpit and that helped tremendously.

On July 11, we saw some debris ahead in the water and sailed over to check it out. It was the butt of a bamboo shoot sticking up. The top went way down into the water. But what caught my attention was the number of nice fish around it. I saw a large Ocean Sunfish swim over and disappear under the keel of the ship followed by an olive drab tripletail. Then two brilliant blue and gold Dorado cruised by like lean, beautiful torpedoes. They were about three feet long. I told Ken to crank the engine and motor us around for another pass while I rigged the rod and reel.

I had salted some small flying fish for bait and put one on the hook and dropped it over as we passed close to the tree. A small jack hit it instantly and I hauled him in, hooked on another bait and threw out again and promptly caught another foot long jack. We had enough fish but I really wanted a Dorado so made another circle of the bamboo. The sails were still up but the wind being light we had been able to simply power around the fishing hole. Suddenly there was a rain squall upon us and the sails filled and we took off, naturally at that precise moment the Dorado took the bait and I set the hook. The sting of the hook surprised the fish and it shot up into the air, shaking its body into a blur. When it hit the water it took off on a run that made the reel scream! We were sailing fast and the combination of that, plus the speed of the fish was too much for the line and it parted, POW! I saw the fish jump once more and I was sorry that I had burdened it with the hook and line that streamed from its mouth.

By the time the squall left us rolling in the swell we were far away from the bamboo, so continued on our course for the Bahamas. I took a knife, cleaned and filleted the fish, and got busy cooking while they were still fresh. To be sure, they were much appreciated and a welcome change to our bland fare.

The next morning there was not a hint of a breeze blowing. I cranked the engine at 5:45 and began motoring. At sunup a third tropic bird joined us and they took turns watching and diving at the log rotor spinning off the miles astern, or trying to alight on the masthead or spreaders. They would spend hours at this and finally get so tired they would all land in the water and apparently talk over their lack of success, but pretty soon they would be at it again.

I was getting breakfast when Ken called down and said, "There's a funny looking ship up ahead with a submarine out in front and the conning tower is painted day-glow red." I had seen that rig come into Savannah many times and handed up the binoculars, asking him if it didn't look more like a tug, towing a pointed-bow, seagoing barge (which does in fact look like the bare hull of a ship). After a long look he concurred, "Yep that's what it is."

They use the rig to haul cement from down South to Savannah. I'd watched it come in and out of Savannah while fishing and shrimping off Daufuskie. And when going over the Talmadge Bridge in Savannah I would see it tied up next to the tall silos across from the city. I could never figure out the economy of it all, but I'm sure there is a good reason for using that particular system.

Ken and I took turns at the helm. There was not enough breeze to even move the wind vane on *Hazel*, much less to push the ship. The engine thumped out the miles and heated up the cabin, but we had to keep moving. This was not the time or the place to tarry.

The wind vane kept swinging around so I took a bit of nylon string and tied it to the pushpit railing. That made it behave itself. I think *Hazel* was bored with it all.

I spent an hour on the bow rail peering into the beautiful blue water of the Atlantic. I saw all sorts of flotsam and jetsam. Like a green mangrove pod, a plastic coffee cup with goose neck barnacles clinging to its frail side (having apparently crossed the ocean). Some clear strips of plastic material. Globs of oil or tar—probably pumped out of a ship's bilge, and lots of small fry. I couldn't tell what kind of fish they were. Most of the stuff I saw reminded me of land. We were getting close. I felt a bit sad really, that this very enjoyable leg of our journey was winding down.

Up ahead I saw a large black oval shape in the water and directed Ken to alter course and pass close by it. As we drew near I saw that it was a ball of tar about three feet in diameter. It barely floated, and was clean of any barnacles or crabs but there were fish around it and another olive-drab, tripletail swam over to the ship. I saw some more of the golden ones too and went below to rig the pole.

Ken shoved the helm hard over, for another pass. There was a loud crack, and the counterweight on the wind vane broke right off and hung by the piece of line I had tied it to the railing with. I had forgotten about it in the excitement of the kill. Well, it was out of harm's way now. The tripletail swam quickly back to his lump of tar.

I baited the hook with a small salted flying fish and as we passed close by the tarball I gave it to the fish and he took it. I played out about 10 feet of line, and then set the hook. The fish took a run around the tarball and broke the line! That really upset me. I wanted some nice, big, juicy fillets.

I quickly put on my homemade lure and wham! One of the Dorado took the hook and the fight was on. It was not a large fish, only five or six pounds; but it gave quite a battle with spectacular jumps and long fast runs. It finally tired and I heaved it aboard and put the lure back over and immediately caught another about the same size. I put the pole away and watched as the dying fish turned from a beautiful, blue and gold to the silvery sheen of death. The change took only seconds following their final quiver, but such is life. I took the knife and cut the fillets off and threw the carcasses overboard. Something else would dine this day.

The flesh of the Dorado or *Dolphinfish* is white and delicate of flavor. I cut it in chunks, salt and peppered it, then rolled it in flour before deep-frying it. This gave us a big plate of tasty fish to dip into whenever the whim struck. It also keeps well if left on top of the stove where the air can circulate over it. This is my favorite fish.

I spent the rest of the afternoon gluing and screwing backup plates over the broken counterweight arm. It was simple to fix and was stronger than the original when I'd finally bolted it back to the vane. I had learned another hard lesson in the process…never tie *Hazel* down.

The little Volvo thumped on through the day and on into the night. During my early watch I noticed the loom of a town to the West-Southwest. When I called Ken out for his trick, I showed it to him and asked that he keep a good watch and to call me should he see or hear anything unusual.

Two hours later Ken called me and said that there were lights ahead. I took a look through the binoculars and affirmed that we were in sight of land. After checking the chart and our DR position we decided that it was Eleuthera. We had over-corrected and were about half way down the island. We changed course to run North and stayed well off shore. All these islands are dangerous to approach in the dark. I turned in for some sleep and came out again for my watch at 4:00 AM.

We were still under power and thumped along the front of Eleuthera as the sun came up. And there was land for the first time in twenty-eight days. Ken roused out at 8:00 AM and I got breakfast going; grits and eggs with cold dolphin. It went down real good. (I oft times wonder if grits would not be more widely used as a staple food if they had been named pinole, ground maize, corn bits or the like, because it is basically and totally ground corn). After wash-up I got on the charts and began to lay out our approach to Nassau and to read over the description of the harbour entrance, etc.

At 9:30 a light land breeze came up but only enough to keep the sails taut and the ship from rolling. We kept the engine going so we could make Nassau before nightfall.

Our noon line of position cut right through Egg Island, (a half-mile to our port), as we rounded the North end of Eleuthera and set our course for the entrance to Nassau Harbour. At 3 PM a nice, strong breeze came up and we shut the engine down. It had run steady as a heartbeat for over thirty hours. I dipped the tank and computed our fuel consumption at one-quart-per-hour, at five knots. I was happy with that.

We sailed the last three hours, taking the sails down at 6 PM just off the jetty at Nassau Harbour. It had taken twenty-eight days, seven hours and forty-five minutes. The log read 3,612.9 nautical miles. WE MADE IT!

Ken cranked the engine while I stowed the sails and tidied up the ship. We both bathed and put on clean clothes. Earlier on I had hoisted the yellow "Q" flag and put the US flag at the stern. We wanted to look neat and sharp for our visit.

Ken had been to Nassau several years prior in a powerboat and knew his way around so I let him take over and steer for the Nassau Harbour Club down past the bridge. But when it came time to dock he was relieved to hand the helm over to me. I backed into a slip while Ken put lines out to the piling on either side of the bow and ran two stern lines out. At 8 PM I shut the little Volvo down. We had indeed and for sure made it.

Ken disappeared inside the building adjacent to the quay and I finished up the log, my journal and just sat quietly letting my mind and body sense the moment. It was not an anti-climax, nor was it a rockets going off event either, but I was not as exhilarated as I thought I'd be. I was sorry that it was over and wished that I didn't have to come in from the sea. It was a very nice and orderly world out there. There were no stop signs, taxes or crime. No hopeless social/economic problems. It was clean and fresh and organized. It was diametrically opposite to what lay just ten feet away. But that is not the way it is, and we were back…now it was time to come forth and face the real world.

The sound of voices with the lilt of the Bahamas and Ken's deep Southern drawl brought me up and I put the books away and went out into the cockpit and met the two

Bahamas Landfall 177

agents as they came aboard. They were very professional with a warm tint that made the usual ordeal seem almost pleasant. We filled in the various forms, which they signed and stamped. Then they stamped our passports and we were cleared. They told us that we should take down the "Q" flag and asked if we had a courtesy flag. I did and said that I'd hoist it immediately. While Ken showed them off the ship I changed the flags showing that we were officially and legally in the Bahamas.

Ken got his kit together, he would stay ashore in the hotel, and I would stay with the ship. He had called Sally, his wife and she would fly down the next day, and join us for the trip home.

We went to the hotel where I ordered a hamburger and french fries and a big double dip ice cream cone for dessert. Then we took a walk along the busy street of Nassau, to get our land legs back.

I found it difficult to walk a straight line for the first few hours ashore; one tends to tack off at odd angles, bump into people and generally act a bit tipsy. After thinking about this I decided that for the past month we had basically been using the 3-point stance. We always had a hand on the ship and did not rely all that much on balance and especially when below because there was just not enough room to stand on your own two stems with the ship rolling. But by walking around as much as possible, the natural balance and order returns.

We had a drink in the bar and I headed back to the ship. It had been a very long day and I was bone tired. I don't think I awoke once during the night but when I awoke the next morning the bright lights along the quay startled me. I thought we were about to be hit with a ship or running aground. It really gave me a start and my heart was pounding when I stuck my head up and saw that we were tied to the quay.

Sally blew in like a fresh breeze and was as delighted to see us as we were to see her. She was a long legged brunette and was a joy to be around. She also was a good sailor and an excellent cook. I was really looking forward to the improved galley fare on the way home for she volunteered to be the ships cook.

Ron Barnes, a mutual friend of ours from Brunswick, Georgia had flown down with Sally for a day or two of sun and fun. We all went to town and had good noisy meals, and went snorkeling together. We went sailing several times with a family we'd met from Chicago. It was good to be back among friendly fun loving people. We had a grand time of it, but once again and all too soon, it was time to let go, and move on to the next adventure.

On July 20 we made one last raid on the town, brought it all down to the ship and stowed it. Next we filled the fuel and water tanks and after paying our bill at the hotel, untied *Blue Gipsy* and motored out under the bridge to the breakwater. We were homeward bound but would cruise the Berry Islands on the way. We had all thoroughly enjoyed our stay in Nassau.

CHAPTER SIXTEEN
Turn Right to Home

I put the jenny on and hoisted the mains'l. *Blue Gipsy* responded like a filly. She seemed happy to be away from the confines of the harbour and was ready for a romp at sea, but it didn't last long. The further we got from Nassau the lighter the wind fell until we were barely sailing at all. It was a beautiful day though, and we were in no real hurry. We plodded along and enjoyed the leisurely pace.

    I trailed a lure but had no luck, and at 1800, took it in. We had arrived at Little Whale Key and would anchor for the night. I put two hooks down, then donned mast, snorkel and fins and jumped over the side into the sparkling clear water. A green lawn of eel grass disappeared in the hazy distance and I had to work the points of the plow anchors down through the crust of coral sediment and grass roots. But it was worth the effort and I knew if the wind picked up during the night that I'd be able to simply roll over and go back to sleep.

    I was burying the point of the second plow when a movement caught my attention and a five foot shark was suddenly in full view about fifty feet away. It was moving at a hunting pace and had undoubtedly heard the commotion of my activities and had come to investigate. I finished my task and made my way back to the ship and aboard.

I'm not afraid of sharks but from experience I know that they are unpredictable and should not be trusted. The more of them there are, the more likely they are to give trouble. I only saw the one and kept a wary eye on it.

On the way back to the ship I saw some beautiful fighting conchs on the bottom. I stopped long enough to collect a few. They are good eating and their shells would make nice mementos of the trip. The shark was nowhere to be seen.

Back aboard we found that one of the conchs had a small fish pinned under its mantle and it was just what I needed, some bait. I cut it up in small pieces and rigged hand lines, and we all started fishing. Ken caught a nice Yellowtail Snapper and Sally caught a Pigfish. Then Ken caught another Yellowtail. I caught a small smooth Dogfish (like a small shark). By then the bait was gone and we had enough fish for dinner so we quit, and while I cleaned the fish Sally got the skillet hot. It sure was nice to have such a good-looking cook aboard.

We enjoyed the meal. Afterwards I washed up and we all went topside for a sundowner. It was a beautiful, calm night and the stars were brilliant. We talked about the voyage, filling Sally in on all the exciting things that had happened to us, and about Nassau and the rest of the trip home. We also decided to sail to Little Stirrup Key the next day. The mosquitoes moved in, so we moved in too, and went to bed. I took the quarter berth, Ken and Sally the twin berths forward.

After a good nights sleep we got up and had a toast and coffee breakfast. Afterwards, we got the anchors aboard and sailed away. It was 9:30 and we only had about thirty-odd miles to go so we were not in a hurry. I had the jenny and full main pulling, but the fisherman breeze gradually died and we were once again using the engine. We didn't mind. All sense of urgency was gone and we could relax and simply enjoy ourselves.

We put the hooks down at 5:30 and I dove over and set them both, then took my spear gun and went hunting for supper. The water was crystal clear and there were plenty of fish around. I saw a great barracuda next to a small ledge of coral getting cleaned up. He had turned a tarnished silvery black. Small fish, only an inch or so long, swarmed all around it, picking off the various parasites they found. It was a remarkable sight. I didn't intrude on the sanctity of the place, it was neutral ground.

A bit further on I saw another small ledge and a number of Snapper and Grouper in the shadows under the edge. I picked out a nice grouper and speared it. I immediately made my way back to the ship. I wanted nothing to do with a four or five foot Barracuda.

I handed the fish up to Ken and he put it in the bucket. There was still plenty of daylight and I was enjoying the snorkeling so much, I went back down by the cleaning station to see if any other big fish had dropped by. As I was approaching the ridge, my eye caught the outline of something remarkable; the small ridge was part of an old ship. I could see the rest of it along the bottom. Because of the angle of the sun it had been too faint to detect earlier. I swam around trying to get a better idea of how big the ship had been. I looked to where the mast would have been and there on the bottom was a pile of belaying pins! I couldn't believe my eyes! These are usually the first items that divers pick up, so the wreck had never been found or dove on. Was she a treasure ship, a slaver? I probably will never know for the coral had encapsulated it into a rocky mass that would take heavy equipment to get through. I picked up four of the belaying pins and what looked to be an iron hook and took them back to the ship and handed them up to Ken.

I put them in another bucket and cleaned the fish. After supper I took the fish head and put it on a heavy line for bait and threw it over to see what would take it. It didn't take long before I hooked a large fish and after a lengthy fight had a five-foot shark on the surface. I took one of the belaying pins and smacked it on the head. The pin broke in half but it stunned the shark long enough for me to remove the hook. I'd had enough of that so quit with it. The day was rapidly drawing to a glorious close and it was time for our sundowner.

We had our cocktails sitting on top of the cabin talking when we noticed a glowing mass coming up from the depths below. We watched in fascination as a small organism came to the surface and suddenly turned into a pinwheel of green effervescence. I got the flashlight and flipped it on the pinwheel...it was a compact, worm-like creature about an inch long. It was swimming in a tight circle while emitting a constant stream of bright greenish light. Then there were hundreds of them all around the ship. What a sight! We had never seen the likes of this...it continued the entire time we were out. Once again the breeze fell light, the mosquitoes moved in and we retired below.

The next morning we got an early start; there would be no more stops until we arrived home. As we were pulling out into deeper water I saw a tabletop coral formation with a great school of Red Snapper hovering close by. Several nice Grouper eased along toward the safety of the coral. I would really have liked to stop and fish a while but it was time to move on.

The wind was flunky so we chugged, flopped and banged along. By nightfall we were off Pinder Point but couldn't pick the light out of all the background lights from Freeport, so we continued to motor sail on and picked up the Gulf Stream. We kept on a Westerly course until we could see the bright loom of lights at Palm Beach...then we turned right for home.

July 23, 1971...

We had been running the engine for over thirty-six hours. According to the navigation we were a bit East of the Gulf Stream, so put a more Westerly course correction in and continued on. A thick band of thunderheads marked the stream and we were soon in the middle of them. That morning I watched a frigate bird rob a greater tern of its catch. Such powerful fliers they are and able to match the frantic gyrations of the smaller bird until it dropped its catch...which was snapped up before it hit the water.

The wind finally picked up out of the East and we shut the engine down. I was very tired because I had been up and down most of the night navigating, looking for ships and running sails up and down as a breeze came up or dropped off. I turned in for a nap. An hour later Sally called me out and said that Ken needed help with the sails.

I made my way topside and took in the situation at a glance. A great thunderstorm was just to the West of us and the wind had suddenly shifted backing the jenny and the ship simply stopped.

On the way to the foredeck I shouted for Ken to start the engine and power us around so the jenny would fill and I could get the whisker pole off without breaking anything. For some reason he threw off the jib sheet...I jumped behind the mast as the pole went up through the rigging, breaking off the lower end and tangling itself in the port shrouds. I got it all down and while doing that, had Ken steer us on a Northeast course away from the storm. Then I put up the working jib and reefed the main. The wind had picked up considerably. With the sails pulling hard and the stream taking us North, we were soon out of danger. The wind let up and I once again set the jenny. No pole this time. I inspected the broken pole and found only the "U" shaped part of the end had been carried away. I could still use it by sticking the protruding latch pin through the clew cringle. As long as I kept plenty of tension on the jib sheet and the preventor running forward, it would stay put.

The motor ship *Campeche* out of Veracruz came by for a look. We gave them a friendly wave and the crew lining the deck waved back. I'm sure the bikini clad Sally made their day. They moved on and I went below and managed a ragged hour's sleep in the hot cabin. This coastwise stuff was getting me down.

I came on watch and took over the ship. Thundersqualls were all about like dirty puffs of popcorn. We were motor sailing, trying to dodge between the worst of them, and actually doing pretty good. We carried on through the night.

I turned in at midnight and came on again at 4:00 AM Conditions were about the same except for an ominous dark cloud that was slowly overtaking us from astern. I kept my eye on it and steered a more Westerly course to maneuver out of harm's way. I almost made it but decided to douse the sail before that sudden reversal of the wind's direction common to big thunderstorms. I lowered and bagged the working jib and put on the storm jib. Then I furled and secured the mains'l. The wind suddenly shifted one hundred-eighty degrees and picked up to forty or fifty miles-per-hour. The rain beat down in sheets. I sat in the cockpit and kept our heading as best I could. The seas picked up quickly and it was rough going for half an hour. Then the storm moved off…rumbling and grumbling with forks of lightening stabbing down into the water like a great trident. I was glad to be spared and not speared. We were rolling badly with no sail, so up with the jib and main.

Everyone was up and having breakfast by 7:00 AM. It was hot below so we sat around in the coolness of the cockpit and ate from plates on our laps. A large and playful pod of Pilot Whales came by and gave us a moral lift with their exuberant antics. But unlike the porps, these were big creatures and took their play with a bit of…what shall I say; defiance? They seemed to be a little put out by our intrusion and their charges became more aggressive and very close, just missing us as they dove under the bow at the last possible instant. But we still enjoyed them and felt much better for having seen them, but were relieved when they tired of us and moved off.

Somehow I had managed to injure my kneecap and it looked like a goose egg under the skin again. It was not overly painful though and seemed to work all right. I didn't worry about it, it had healed on its own accord once before and it should again.

By now we were about one hundred miles Southeast of the Savannah light tower; our voyage was winding down.

July 25, 1971…

Sally had asked me to awaken her at 0600 so she could

see a sunrise at sea one last time. She brewed us a cup of coffee and while I steered (winds were light and we were again motor-sailing) she sat on the foredeck in jacket and jeans and watched the sun come up. It was a somewhat unsettled day. We still had lots of clouds around but we were moving out of the Gulf stream and they were falling astern.

I took stock of the bird life and saw a couple of white tropic birds and wondered if they were the same ones that had followed us for so many miles. There were also a few of the little black British storm petrels. Sally pointed out a big white bird flying low on the water. It was a snowy egret. A shore bird which had become lost and was over fifty miles at sea and heading further offshore with every wing beat. It was sad to see and there was nothing we could do about it. It seemed not a good omen for the finish of our trip.

The wind picked up and I put the jenny up. Ken came up and complained that I had awakened him. I finally decided that Ken was a motorboater...not a sailor.

I was exhausted and the lost bird we had seen had depressed me. I had just about had it. I was ready to be done with Ken and the trip. But I bit my tongue and turned the helm over to him and took a radio bearing on the Savannah radio beacon. We were on course heading right for it and at 9:00 AM we saw the tower about ten miles away.

We picked up the first sea buoy just past the tower and followed them like a string of pearls up Savannah River. At the jetties we were met by a boatload of Ken's friends.

They passed over a bottle of champagne and we had a toast to a successful trip. It took us the remainder of the day to motor to Thunderbolt Georgia and tie up to a float at the marina. There, we were met by another group of about thirty friends and strangers including the press. Ken's buddies had called them down. It seems that Ken had turned into the adventurer, and I was tagging along. Oh well...it was done.

Customs and immigrations cleared us in but warned me not to move *Blue Gipsy* until import duty had been paid. Since this was Sunday that couldn't happen before the morrow.

My father came up in a runabout and we hugged hello. He was happy to see me and looked great... sunburned and tough looking from shrimping and fishing all summer. He was delighted with *Blue Gipsy*. The crowd drifted away taking Ken and Sally with them. I collected my logbooks and journals, slid the hatch closed and locked it. I took one last long look around, then climbed into the runabout with my father and headed for Daufuskie.

As we swept along at thirty miles an hour, all the familiar rivers and creeks and markers rushed by in a cinema of memories of long ago. I couldn't help but think about it all...how long had it been since my grandfather and my father dreamed this dream...the same dream indeed that I had just awakened from, and found it to be reality. I quite suddenly realized that this particular adventure was over and done...and it had indeed been a long voyage home.

Epilogue

Looking back on the adventure with the eye of a knowledgeable critic I can pick out almost the instant that things took a turn in the wrong direction...and what the proper response should have been. But then, that's what hindsight is all about. That is also how we gain experience so that we don't make the same mistakes again. I should have turned the ship around when the gale hit us coming out of Copenhagen, but I didn't and everything went down hill from there. It just never entered my mind. Even when we got off the beach I was tempted to go forward, toward the goal, not back to the beginning.

    I personally think that the ship held up better than the crew. I was physically and mentally exhausted with the voyage by the time we reached Thunderbolt, Georgia.... Ken was a constant drag on my energy and morale. He really did not want to be on a small sailboat any more, but he was fearful of what his friends would say if he jumped ship. Peer pressure is a real force in most people's lives. It would have been easier on both of us had he left the ship in England. I feel that he almost did but just couldn't make the break. The friendship cooled and I think we both tried very hard not to completely destroy it. I did feel a twinge of regret that the trip had been so demanding. But that is the price we sometimes have to pay for adventure.

Blue Gipsy came through like a trouper. I ordered a new boom and repaired what wear and tear there was. I still own her and we have shared many, many miles and some really exciting adventures. She is a tough little boat and a joy to sail.

I'm very thankful for the time I spent with my grandfather as a child…and for the love of adventure that he passed on to me. I'm thankful too for the practical things that he taught me. I only regret that he didn't have a chance to see the ship and to sail aboard her with my father and me. He would have had a grand time of it. I know my father did. But life goes on.

Being home on Daufuskie was a great healer and I was over it all in a few days. I had to write a big check to cover import duty before I could take *Blue Gipsy* home. I did take the advice of the customs officer who cleared us and turned it all over to a customs broker in Savannah. They cleared her through and I got most of the money refunded.

I tied *Blue Gipsy* to a mooring off my folk's place at Daufuskie and flew back to Saigon. It took a couple of months to clear up loose ends; resign my position with Air America, pack up and ship all my personal belongings back to the States etc., etc. Once that was accomplished I set about in earnest on my next adventure; the 1972 O.S.T.A.R.

I sent in my application and was conditionally accepted, and was issued sail number thirty-seven. The conditions were that I sail at least five hundred miles solo to qualify the ship and me, and then to show up in Plymouth, England far enough in advance of the race for the ship to be inspected. All entrants had to have some special equipment on board, and they wanted to have a look at it, and to make sure the ship and crew were sea worthy.

I had learned a lot the first time around so preparing for the O.S.T.A.R. was much easier. But it did have its own set of problems and that is the stuff that adventures are made of. It is also grist for another mill and hopefully a sequel will follow in the wake of this effort, to tell it the way it was. Good Sailing!